DINOSAUR BRAINS

DINOSAUR BRAINS

Dealing with All Those
Impossible People at Work

ALBERT J. BERNSTEIN, Ph.D.
and Sydney Craft Rozen

WILEY

JOHN WILEY & SONS

New York   *Chichester*   *Brisbane*   *Toronto*   *Singapore*

Library of Congress Cataloging in Publication Data:

Bernstein, Albert J.
    Dinosaur brains: dealing with all those impossible
people at work/ Albert J. Bernstein
and Sydney Craft Rozen.
        p. cm.
    Bibliography: p.
    ISBN 0-471-61808-X
    1. Personnel management.   2. Interpersonal relations.
    3. Job stress. I. Rozen.   Sydney Craft. II. Title.
HF5549.B4518   1989
650.1'3—dc19   88-22336
                                                           CIP

Printed in the United States of America

18 17 16

To Luahna

Contents

Introduction   xiii

Part I: What Is the Dinosaur Brain?   1

Chapter 1:   The Dinosaur Brain and Lizard Logic   3
The Dinosaur Brain metaphor explained, plus the seven principles of Lizard Logic that, to the dinosaur, cover all events and contingencies.

Chapter 2:   How the Dinosaur Brain Works   9
A brief owner's manual for the brain, including directions for use.

Part II: The Rules of Lizard Logic   15

Chapter 3:   Get It Now!   17
Impulsiveness has its uses as a management style, but there are drawbacks too. How to recognize and moderate the "brushfire" approach to your job and cope with the stress-related problems that go with it. Also, working with impulsive people.

Chapter 4:   The Triple F Response: Fight, Flight or Fright   27
Arousing a lizard can lead to aggressiveness, avoidance or immobilization. There's trouble ahead when we try to protect our psyches with defenses that were designed to protect prehistoric beasts.

Chapter 5: Be Dominant! 37
Understanding the rules for social hierarchy at the office. Your Dinosaur Brain can lead you into reflexive competitiveness. Do you really want to go?

Chapter 6: Defend the Territory! 45
To anyone involved in a turf battle at work, the stakes can seem like life and death. The Dinosaur Brain as the basis for the "turf issue." How to cope with territorial colleagues and what to do if you're spending too much time defending your own territory.

Chapter 7: Get the Mate! 57
The predictable patterns of office courtship come from the Dinosaur Brain. Learn to avoid acting like a lovesick lizard if you've lost your heart at work.

Chapter 8: If It Hurts, Hiss! 67
Complaining gets it off your chest—or does it? This collection of blamers and complainers shows you why hissing can be bad for business.

Chapter 9: Like Me, Good; Not Like Me, Bad 77
Lizards see only black and white. Managers must be able to recognize gray. Making too many moral judgments at work can be hazardous to your health.

Part III: Using Lizard Logic 87

Chapter 10: Avoiding the Reptile Response 89
The only real way to win an argument at work is to muzzle your Dinosaur Brain. How to keep the logical part of your brain working, even when you'd rather act like a dinosaur.

Chapter 11: Bad Moods and Internal Television 95
Thoughts are like your own personal internal TV set, but you can decide what to watch. Listings from the Dinosaur Brain Network for prime-time and late-night viewing. Are any of these playing in your head?

Chapter 12: Irritability 99
Working with an irritable lizard can really test your patience. Sometimes the crabby dinosaur might even be you. What happens, and what to do, when the "fight" part of the Triple F Response makes its way to the surface.

Chapter 13: Manipulation 107
Some people use Dinosaur Brain patterns to twist your arm and try to manipulate you into giving them their way. The whole world changes when you learn responses that can make you almost manipulation-proof.

Chapter 14: The Positive Uses of Anger 119
There are times when anger can be a powerful form of communication— as long as you don't adopt it as your basic management style.

Chapter 15: Angry Clients 125
Handling upset clients effectively means keeping them out of their Dinosaur Brains and staying out of yours. Techniques for stopping the verbal fireworks and getting back to solving the client's problem.

Chapter 16: The Customer Service Model 131
Using the Customer Service Model to convince people at both ends of the corporate hierarchy that they're following the same rules and working toward common goals. Protecting the company from the more debilitating effects of the drives for dominance and territory.

Chapter 17: Motivating Yourself and Your Employees 135
Corporate loyalty and motivation arise from a sense of belonging to the herd. A checklist for managers to keep their employees, and themselves, feeling respected, valued and part of the same team.

Chapter 18: Stress Is Not the Enemy 141
People can handle a great deal of stress if they understand the different kinds of tension they'll face at work and follow these coping skills.

Chapter 19: Is Your Mind Out of Shape? 147
The Dinosaur Brain can lead to excitement and enthusiasm—or cognitive sloth and mental flab. Suggestions for a return to mental fitness.

Chapter 20: Long-Term Planning 151
Long-term planning is an alien concept to the Dinosaur Brain, but trying to maintain a career without it is a sure road to extinction. Ideas for infusing some Dinosaur Brain excitement into a dreary cortical task.

Chapter 21: Making Waves 157
Most people are uncomfortable with the kind of tacky self-promotion that's necessary for professional advancement. To keep a career moving forward, the cortex and the Dinosaur Brain have to work together.

Chapter 22: It's Lonely at the Top   165
To the uninitiated, the dinosaurs at the top of the company hierarchy seem part of an Old Boy network. The reality is closer to one lonely old lizard on a hilltop, guarding the herd.

Chapter 23: The Captain Kirk Management Style   171
When an executive takes on too much responsibility as his or her exclusive territory, you get confusion on the Starship Enterprise. Understanding the difference between management and heroics.

Chapter 24: The Mentor Relationship   173
A mentor should not be a parent or a lover but, because of the way the system is set up in many companies, that's what the mentor relationship becomes. Here's why, and what to do about it.

Chapter 25: Why People Get Involved in Office Romances   181
Where else do many professionals find Mr. or Ms. Right if not at the office? How to tell if this is the Real Thing and, if it isn't, what to do to end an office affair with the least possible professional damage.

Chapter 26: How to Save Yourself If Your Company Is "One Big Happy Family"   187
Even the happiest of families have complex and confusing rules about dominance. All too often, it's only the parental figures—the King Lizards—who are happy.

Chapter 27: Corporate Juvenile Delinquents   197
The rules for running a family don't work too well for running a business. If managers act like parents, a lot of people may have to leave home. Management strategies for handling conflict between professional generations.

Chapter 28: Dealing with Old Dinosaurs   207
The office family from the point of view of a rising corporate teenager. Ideas from the Dinosaur Brain for gaining responsibility and independence without getting kicked out of the office.

Chapter 29: Labor and Management   215
The two sides can learn to negotiate, if they avoid their Dinosaur Brains' aggressive streak. Suggestions for enhancing both sides' feelings of corporate affiliation.

Chapter 30: The Customer from Outer Space   221
Most businesses evolve their own languages. To be effective, you have to learn to translate the other person's dialect.

Chapter 31: Gravity 225
Every corporation has its own natural laws that can neither be ignored nor questioned. Fighting against them is like fighting against gravity.

Chapter 32: Habit and Ritual 229
Using rituals to mark important changes at work. The value of ritual objects (washroom keys, corner offices and corporate ties) to the Dinosaur Brain. How to tell if it's a ritual or just a rut.

Chapter 33: Management by Mind-Reading: The Case Against Bad Attitude 237
The Dinosaur Brain's certainty that it knows what is right and wrong is not too far from assuming we can read minds.

Chapter 34: How to Make Your Colleagues Mad at You 241
It's easy—just ignore their Dinosaur Brains. Follow these suggestions and watch the lizards attack.

Afterword 247

Suggested Readings 249

Index 251

Introduction

Whenever I start one of my management seminars, I call everybody in the audience a Dinosaur Brain. Why? Because inside each human brain lurks the brain of a dinosaur—irrational, emotional, easily enraged—waiting to take control.

As a psychologist, I have worked with legions of Dinosaur Brains, and I have realized that humans don't always act like humans. One minute they're normal, rational people; the next, they're little better than reptiles. Trouble comes when they use the Reptile Response —their primitive thinking patterns—instead of the rational part of their brain.

Think about your own job. What was the tension level in the office the last time the boss was on a power trip? Or remember the meeting when hot-headed Bill started ranting and you tried to reason with him, but he just got angrier?

How about the headache you get every time you need computer data and have to deal with game-playing Mary, who insists that your secretary fill out every request in triplicate and sometimes makes you wait a week just for a one-page printout?

Think about how much you dread contract time, when negotiations get bogged down every year by personal vendettas, jurisdictional disputes, imagined slights or out-and-out paranoia.

Who are these Dinosaur Brains? What do they want? How can they not know what they're doing? These are responsible people like you and me, acting out unconscious fantasies of the primeval jungle. Do you stand aside and let them have their way, or do you confront them and risk having your head bitten off?

Why is it that business is business, but when somebody disagrees with you in a meeting, or you get beaten out in a deal, it feels so personal?

Why do people do things to make their jobs so much harder than they need to be? And what can you do when they try to do them to you?

By reading *Dinosaur Brains*, you can learn how to use the wiles of your more highly evolved brain to divert your colleagues from constantly acting out their evolutionary battle and put them back on track. Then everybody can get some work done for a change.

This book deals with irrational thinking and unconscious motivation at the office—because people at work aren't always the rational creatures that other management books talk about. They don't always act in their own best interests, much less in yours.

With practice, it won't be hard for you to stay in control when people around you are overreacting. You can learn the rules and skills for dealing with irrationality in others and gain the self-knowledge to identify and cope with your own Dinosaur Brain behavior.

The secret to dealing with irrational people lies in knowing their rules. Everything people do, no matter how crazy it seems, follows some system of rules. This book is about those rules, which I call Lizard Logic. The rules are primitive and have to do with impulsiveness, survival, dominance, territoriality, sex and aggression. Knowing the rules can make you aware of the warning signs that trigger your own Reptile Response and help you recognize the signals and prevent it or channel it to productive use.

Then I discuss the tactics for getting other people out of their Dinosaur Brain patterns and making them easier to work with. The technique involves creativity—looking at things differently. The problem I see professionally over and over is that people who are creative in other areas don't realize they can use the same creativity in dealing with people at work. This book, and a little reflection, can show you how to tap your creativity to solve office problems.

This book is also about job stress. Life in the lizard lane is very demanding. Usually, it's not the job itself but our emotional response to it that can burn us out and bring on stress-related symptoms: high blood pressure, headaches, ulcers or upset stomach, lower back pain, insomnia or excessive smoking or drinking. This book shows how taming your unconscious can lower your stress level and teaches you ways to keep your cool even when everybody around you has lost control. It tells the secrets of success that you aren't likely to learn in management classes.

Anyone can be a Dinosaur Brain at any time. The Reptile Response happens totally outside of the conscious mind. People aren't aware of it, but it has left countless careers dead in the water. This book will help you deal with the Reptile Response, whether you're a Dinosaur Brain yourself or have to work with one.

There were certainly times during our collaboration on this book when my co-author, Sydney Craft Rozen, and I recognized lizard-like behavior in ourselves or each other. Writing this book has helped us to remember to think before we thrash about.

Sydney is a free-lance editor and writer, with a publishing track record that includes a best-selling get-organized book, and earlier careers as a newspaper writer and college English instructor. Besides sharing the writing duties, she contributed many of the realistic examples of Lizard Logic and irrational behavior that help give our book its personal tone. The book also reflects her writing style, as well as my own.

The concept of Dinosaur Brains and explanations of the psychological principles and self-help techniques that form the basis for the book are mine. Occasional uses of the first person throughout the book refer to me.

Dinosaur Brains is the result of a professional collaboration between Sydney and me that works; a personal appreciation of each other's brontosaurian brilliance; and the intelligent and sensitive support of our spouses, Luahna Ude and Lee Rozen.

And now, to the jungle. . . .

PART I

What Is the Dinosaur Brain?

1

The Dinosaur Brain and Lizard Logic

Consider the dinosaur. It was a masterpiece of design. How could a brain the size of a walnut control a body the size of a tractor-trailer?

Every dinosaur was hatched fully programmed. It knew everything it needed to know: how to stake out a territory, how to handle danger, how to get ahead in the herd, how to find a mate. Being a Mesozoic success was literally all instinct.

Dinosaurs died sixty-five million years ago, but they are still with us—not just in museums and on T-shirts, but on the boards of the Fortune 500. Their bodies might be gone, but their brains, complete with instincts, are the foundations on which our own brains are built.

What is the Dinosaur Brain? Where is it? How does it work? Can it still help us get ahead?

Picture the human brain as an evolutionary sandwich: a cortex (the center of thinking and logic) stacked on top of a dinosaur's brain (instincts and emotions), with a layer called the limbic system in between.

The Dinosaur Brain is our source of instructions for handling instincts and emotions as old as the dinosaurs: aggression and anger, mating and sexual attraction, territoriality and fear, social hierarchy and loyalty.

The cortex is the part of our brain that makes us human. It is the area in which thinking, associating, reasoning and logic occur. When the Dinosaur Brain gets in the way of rational, organized, businesslike thinking, the result can be like trying to reason with a lizard.

The patterns in the Dinosaur Brain can be divided into seven specific rules that I call Lizard Logic. To the dinosaur, they cover all events and contingencies. We look at each principle in depth in later chapters, but here is a short course in reptilian rationalizing.

Get It Now! Impulsiveness

More than anything else, reptiles can't wait. All Lizard Logic patterns are immediate. Dinosaur Brain thinking is short term, with high emotional involvement. Dinosaur Brain managers are always putting out brushfires and never finding time for long-term planning. Their arousal systems are going full time, producing chaos for co-workers, not to mention stress-related symptoms such as ulcers, headaches, upset stomach, insomnia and maybe excessive smoking or drinking.

Bill is a high-energy guy. He thinks fast and gets people motivated, but he's a little slow on follow-through. Unless his subordinates pick up the ball, nothing gets done. Bill is happiest when he's running around, making contacts and putting out fires. He's always starting new systems, but he doesn't stay around long enough to see that they run. His subordinates wish he would give them more guidance and support.

At meetings Bill tends to cut people off because he already knows what they're going to say. He tends to jump to conclusions and often has to eat his words. Bill is obviously bright, and upper management likes his energy and enthusiasm. But he won't get promoted until he learns to control his impulsiveness.

Fight, Run or Freeze

Dinosaurs have three ways of responding to threat or aggression. They fight back; they run away; or sometimes the arousal gets so high that they become completely immobile, unable to think or function. When people are "stressed out," we can see the three Dinosaur Brain patterns most clearly.

Fred is used to getting the highest rating on his job reviews. But this time he is rated "Fair" on a particular trait and considers it an attack. He yells at his boss and threatens a lawsuit if his rating isn't changed to "Excellent."

Fred's Dinosaur Brain is screaming, "Fight!" and he doesn't see that his raving will damage his career more than a whole page of "Fair" ratings.

Stress builds up in Carolyn's department; she calls in and takes a "mental health day." She hopes if she stays away, somebody else will handle it. It's not that she's irresponsible, just overwhelmed.

Carolyn's Dinosaur Brain tells her that flight is a solution. She doesn't see that the problems will compound while she's gone.

George is in a meeting, presenting his plan, when he's asked a couple of on-target questions. When he opens his mouth to answer, no sound comes out. He's lost his voice and his mind is blank.

Stage fright is a good example of the immobilizing power of the Dinosaur Brain.

Be Dominant! Hierarchies, Dominance and Power Struggles

Reptiles love social hierarchies, and they always seem to be trying to demonstrate that they are the top dinosaur, no matter what the organizational chart says. They often get into trouble by getting involved in power struggles with anyone and everyone. Consider this exchange:

"The planning meeting will be at 10 A.M. in my office," announces the first vice-president.

"Sorry, but I can't possibly make it until 2. And, since I have to present all the sketches, it'll be easier just to meet in my office," says the second vice-president.

So the executives reschedule. But at 1:30 an "emergency" comes up for the first vice-president. The two o'clock session is impossible, of course. So, he tells his secretary, "Just call everybody and set things up for 4 P.M. right here. I'm so jammed up, I won't even be able to leave my desk."

Each vice-president is trying to assert dominance. The reptilian response here is to appear more important by being busier or more in demand. Each executive wants to gain control over when the meeting will occur, because that control is a symbol of who is the most important. When this is done with style, it's called one-upsmanship. Without style, it is merely petty. The purpose of the meeting may be lost in the maneuvering to be on top.

Defend the Territory! Power and Empire-Building

This turf issue is classic. When a lizard's territory is broached, he or she will become agitated and use a number of behaviors to try to scare off, intimidate or possibly destroy the intruder. The best way to deal with territorial issues is head-on, but not through confrontation.

Doctors, for example, learn very early that if they come on a medical floor and don't speak to the head nurse, their time on that floor is going to be much more difficult. Likewise, if you're in someone else's part of the building and there's a chance that the person behaves territorially, call beforehand and identify your reason for being there, or stop by the person's office and say what you're doing there and how long you plan to stay.

The biggest problem people seem to have with territory-defenders is not taking their territoriality seriously enough and prodding at the boundaries. You may think defending a territory is silly, but to the person who does it, it's life itself.

Get the Mate! Office Romances

When lizards see an attractive member of the opposite sex, they immediately behave in courtship patterns instead of paying attention to business. This can lead to a wonderful relationship, but more often it can result in inappropriate, annoying behavior, sexual harassment or unwanted office romances.

David and Laura started meeting for a drink after work every night to discuss the project they were working on. One night the drink led to dinner, then dancing, and the next morning David and Laura took the same cab to the office. Now they meet for lunch every day, call each other's extensions just to whisper "I love you," giggle when they "accidentally" meet at the coffee machine and send each other cute messages through interoffice mail. They think everybody else thinks their relationship is as wonderful as they do. Their supervisor wonders when they're getting any work done.

David and Laura don't know that they're following a pattern seventy million years old. They think they invented it. The Dinosaur Brain is in charge of mating, and it has its own ways of going about courtship. Office romances can be a problem if you don't understand the Reptile Response patterns involved.

If It Hurts, Hiss! Complaining and Placing Blame

The dinosaur never sees himself as the source of any of his troubles. Whenever something goes wrong, he has two responses: to complain or to blame. He's always eager to compare notes with fellow sufferers and to defend himself from any criticism. Consider these two examples:

Complaining. *A group of co-workers goes to a nearby bar after work and plays "Can You Believe How Messed Up This Company Is?" They go home feeling a little better, but over the long haul, their morale drops even lower.*

Blaming. *Sally is never wrong. No matter what happens, she can tell you whose fault it was. Her supervisor didn't tell her what to do; her employees won't listen or God has singled her out for punishment. She'll enthusiast-*

ically explain with great concern and conviction how other people make it impossible for her to do anything.

Dinosaurs were very vocal about their pain, which served to warn the herd about danger or to summon aid. At the office, hissing might have other effects.

Like Me, Good; Not Like Me, Bad

Dinosaurs always divide the world into two categories: good and evil. Good is, of course, people like them. Often, decisions that should be made on the merits of the case are made instead on reflexive moral judgments. At their worst, these judgments can turn into paranoia.

Charles turned thumbs down on young Brown's request for promotion. The official reason was that Brown lacked management experience. Brown is gay, but some of Charles's best friends are gay. There were other things. True, the boy was bright, and everybody kept harping on how "creative" he was. But there was something . . . not his sexual preference, surely. . . . Charles couldn't quite put a finger on it. Brown appeared, well, maybe a bit too "dramatic."

Charles's Dinosaur Brain reacted in an automatic, negative way to someone who was unlike him. Only later did his mind search for reasons that Brown's differences might make him unsuitable for the promotion. As we can clearly see in this case, the Dinosaur Brain is the source of all prejudice and discrimination.

In the lizard world, you are either a part of the herd, a predator, or prey. There is no middle ground and no gray at all.

The Dinosaur Brain operates outside of consciousness, but with practice, you can tell when it is in control. In Chapter 2 you'll find out how.

2

How the Dinosaur Brain Works

To understand how the brain works, let's pretend that there are two little managers inside the head. Each manager corresponds to one of the two parts of the brain, one to the cortex and the other to the Dinosaur Brain. (We're omitting the limbic system. For ease of understanding, most of its function is included in the role of the Dinosaur Brain.) Each manager's job description is the same: See that the body does whatever it needs to do to ensure survival and happiness.

The first manager, Cortex, is reasonable, resourceful and, at times, a bit dull. He wears the kind of career suit you read about in *Dress for Success*. In Cortex's office, stacked to the ceiling, is a huge collection of textbooks, records of previous experiences, commentaries, management books and motivational tapes. His desk drawers are full of notes to himself and lists of things to do. All of these instructions are authoritative and encompassing, but they can also be dry, and, like the real world, are incomplete, contradictory and confusing.

The second executive, Dinosaur, can be a flamboyant rabble-rouser as he paces his office, resplendent in a plaid sports jacket. He's capable of stirring things up at a second's notice. His office is dec-

orated with photos of him shaking hands with famous people, pin-ups, cartoons, gnawed bones and unwashed coffee cups, as well as a few items of surprising beauty and simplicity. On his walls are framed sales awards; in a drawer are his piles of reprimands.

Dinosaur has been around for millions of years, but his management book is a single volume: one short policies and procedures manual that covers everything. It is direct, to the point, and sometimes wrong.

These two managers are inside us in the two parts of our brain. They could accomplish quite a bit if they worked as a team, but usually they can't get along. Sometimes, like Cortex, we work logically and rationally. Sometimes, like Dinosaur, our style is provocative, inspired and emotional. Let's take a look at how we actually experience these conflicting parts, the cortex and the Dinosaur Brain, to see how we can become more aware of them.

Unconscious Motivation

Many theorists have speculated about what is in the unconscious and how it works. Freud thought it was full of animal nature, repressed sexual, aggressive material and such. Jung thought it contained a collective way of viewing the world. Maybe both were right. The unconscious is less full of events than patterns for perceiving the world. At the very base are the Dinosaur Brain's rituals, which are present in all of us. Above that are patterns we learn in growing up and throughout our lives.

To understand what's in the unconscious, we must know how it works. There is too much information in any situation. We can't perceive it all, so we need to have some way to focus on what's important. This is called the *cognitive set* and is really like a collection of pointers. We are not aware of the pointers so much as of what they point at. The unconscious works through cognitive set, directing our attention toward some things and away from others. Usually these are the things we have to notice or avoid noticing in order to survive physically and emotionally.

Included within the Dinosaur Brain part of our unconscious are instructions to focus on basic survival situations:

"Protect yourself, fight back or run away" (Anger);

"Intruder in the territory; do something" (Danger);

"Possible sex object; show off" (Sexuality);

"Displeased father figure; appease immediately" (Fear).

We dress up these instructions with grammar and syntax, because that's the only way we can talk about them. They are really visceral rather than verbal. We come to know them by their effects, repetitious patterns of thoughts and behavior.

When your Dinosaur Brain is in control, your thoughts and actions seem so right, so natural, so much like the real you because they're preprogrammed, and they come from inside. You don't feel the shift from human thinking to dinosaur thinking; you just do what the Dinosaur Brain wants. Since they happen outside your consciousness, there is no way to experience the choices the Dinosaur Brain makes. Only the results of those choices are apparent. This is the basis of what psychologists call unconscious motivation: doing things for reasons of which you aren't aware.

I call the Dinosaur Brain's unconscious decisions the Reptile Response. People do not choose to make them, nor do they arrive at them through thinking. They are already there. We make situations fit their basic structure. They are ritualistic, that is, complex and patterned, and they include ways of seeing, feeling and acting that all go together.

These patterns also defy logic. People explaining their Reptile Responses fall back on saying that certain things are "just true" and will attack you for questioning them. Dinosaur Brain thinking is accompanied by high emotional arousal and consequent impairment of rational reasoning. It isn't logical, but a lot of force and conviction are behind it.

These unconscious patterns are a part of everyone's psychological makeup, not just that of the guy down the hall. They underlie conscious thinking. If the cortex is turned off or down by drugs (including caffeine), fatigue or emotion, anyone can start acting like a dinosaur.

Most books about management and self-improvement don't take unconscious motivation into account. They assume that if you want to do something, you just get up and do it. They avoid talking about what happens when what you're trying to do conflicts with what is already in your unconscious.

Business decisions should be based on logic rather than emotion. They can be tempered by emotion but should not be primarily emotional. Most people, however, don't know how to recognize the difference. Emotional decisions most often occur in recognizable patterns. They follow Lizard Logic rules. You can see other people following these rules every day at work, but can you also see yourself?

How many times have you vowed that you'll set aside time for long-range planning? Have you promised yourself that this time you'll control your temper at the staff meeting? How do you feel when an employee goes over your head to get a decision changed? How do you react when somebody calls you by the wrong title? What's the attraction that makes you walk by the office of the cute manager on the twenty-third floor? Why does your mind blank out during a presentation, when you knew what you were going to say before you walked into the conference room? Why can you criticize your company at the daily coffee break but bristle with loyalty when somebody from the outside takes a verbal jab at your boss? We see such evidence of unconscious motivation every day.

You need choice and control in dealing with Dinosaur Brain responses in yourself and others. You will gain control over your behavior at work by recognizing Lizard Logic and using your cortex to choose another, more professional response.

Now let's take a more in-depth look at how those two managers, Cortex and Dinosaur Brain, work.

Instincts and Emotions

Instincts are complex patterns of behavior that are "wired in" to the system. Birds who have never flown south can successfully migrate thousands of miles and return to the same spot; all reptiles do battle in the same way. In the human brain, these instinctive patterns, dealing with anger, fear, sex, territory and social hierarchies, are very likely to be expressed every day on the job. Even though they usually don't lead to success, they seem so right, so natural, because they come from inside. They are the unconscious programs that make us leave the office shaking our heads and asking ourselves, "Why did I do that?"

We experience much of the brain's activity in the body rather than in the head. Emotions, for example, are triggered by the brain but cause changes in muscles, hormones and bodily organs. Remember the rush of feeling when you got that promotion? You didn't experience that in words or pictures; it was somewhere in your body. Those visceral cues are Dinosaur's main management tool.

In the long run, the cortex can control the Dinosaur Brain because the cortex is smarter, but it has to deal with confusion, indecision and contradictions. The Dinosaur Brain, like former White House Chief of Staff Alexander Haig, is apt to announce, "I'm in control here," especially in situations that involve the presence of threat, territory or sex.

People can turn on a Dinosaur response automatically when certain things happen. You can recognize the response by its battle cry: "Get out of the way. I know how to handle this." This reaction is sometimes necessary in a crisis, but the Dinosaur Brain can turn everything into a crisis. This technique is often known as brushfire management.

Ethologists, people who study instincts, call stimuli that bring on instinctive patterns *releasers*. The most powerful releaser is seeing or hearing other people act according to Reptile Response patterns —the Dinosaur Brain at work.

Godzilla Meets Rodan

Dinosaur patterns are provocative. Seeing someone else lose his or her temper or begin an obvious power play can pull you right into your Dinosaur Brain too, leading to what is unscientifically known as the Godzilla meets Rodan effect: There is a great deal of sound and fury; buildings shake, but very little gets accomplished.

Here are some provocative statements. When you hear people say them, you'll know that, even though they may think they're behaving rationally, their Dinosaur Brains are not far behind:

> "I just want to tell you my *real* feelings about. . . ."
>
> "You always. . . ."
>
> "You never. . . ."
>
> "I checked with Joe and Mary, and we *all* feel. . . ."
>
> "Why wasn't I consulted about . . . ?"
>
> "How come some people are allowed to . . . ?"
>
> "I thought *I* was in charge. . . ."
>
> "In this company we do things certain ways. . . ."
>
> "In the good old days. . . ."

In the business world, attacks are not usually launched with teeth and claws: They begin instead with statements similar to those above. When you hear these kinds of statements, you know you're in for a particular kind of conversation. They may sound like a question, comment or opinion, but your Dinosaur Brain recognizes them as attacks. If you do nothing to stop it, it will be your Dinosaur Brain that responds, "Get out of the way, Cortex, I'm in control."

PART **II**

The Rules of Lizard Logic

3

Get It Now!

A triceratops lives on the rim of an immense valley. Before him are magnificent vistas, exciting new things to eat, water, shelter—a paradise. He's on his way. As he lumbers along, he's continually distracted. A scent here, a clump of grass, a fight. The valley is full of promise, but the future will have to wait. There's just too much going on right now.

Decisions are easy for a dinosaur. If it's food, eat it. If it's an enemy, kill it or run away. Every creature or object is either dealt with immediately or ignored. More than anything else, reptiles can't wait. All Lizard Logic patterns are immediate. Dinosaur Brain thinking is always short-term, with high emotional involvement.

Managers with Dinosaur Brain syndrome spend most of their time putting out brushfires and never find time for long-range planning. All of their arousal systems are going full time, producing stress-related complaints.

Ah, but the excitement! The impulsive life has much to recommend it: nonstop action, no ambiguity, no wasted effort. It's the meat and potatoes of existence, with no broccoli. As a management style, it has its uses, but there are drawbacks as well.

Impulsive managers work on a series of highs: high energy, high arousal, high enthusiasm. They are 100 percent behind what they do and aren't afraid to speak out when they have an opinion. They inspire other people and get themselves and others moving. They can be just the right medicine for a department that's bogged down with stick-in-the-muds who question every decision and are suspicious of every change.

Impulsive managers should learn to delegate, though, because they tend to lose interest very quickly. They're great sprinters, but have no strength or interest in the long pull. Follow-through isn't their strong suit, and they're best suited to short-term assignments as, for instance, a department's sparkplug or builder of morale and enthusiasm. Then, when things are running smoothly, they can move on and accept a new challenge.

Clarity and Directness

Dinosaur Brain managers have an amazing ability to get to the heart of the matter. The problem is, so many matters have more than one heart. Sometimes an impulsive supervisor's priorities are wrong and attention goes to whatever is loudest or brightest, rather than what's most important.

These managers tend to have major problems balancing different roles in their lives, for instance as businesspeople, committee members, spouses and parents. They try to do the interesting or compelling part of each role all the time, but when it's not interesting or if it's painful, they can usually find a competing emergency.

Molly is a go-getter. She makes decisions easily and quickly. Luckily for her, she's bright and her decisions are usually correct. Sometimes, though, she opens her mouth and inserts her foot.

It's easy to get caught up in Molly's excitement as you listen to her talk about all the wonderful things she'll do and how quickly she'll do them. It's not that she lies, because she sincerely thinks that what she's promising to do is important and will be fun. There just aren't enough hours in the day for her. At first, you're impressed with her energy, but when you find out that she hasn't followed through, you begin to be wary of what she says.

Molly has trouble balancing her roles at work and outside it. Her personal life has been a series of unsatisfying relationships that always seem great at the beginning, but she just never has the time to make them into anything permanent. If she's failing in love, her job suffers at the same time, but when people start threatening her at work, her new boyfriend has to wait.

Boredom and Impatience

The hardest thing for impulsive managers to tackle is the day-to-day grind. They tend to cut people off in mid-sentence because they "already know" what people are going to say. Impulsive lizards would rather be doing than talking. They just can't tolerate boredom. The trouble is, in our society, civilized people have to be able to withstand a great deal of boredom. Impulsive people can't do this. When things are running smoothly, they tend to start brushfires so they can have something exciting to do.

These people are often adrenaline junkies, or possibly worse. Sometimes they use drugs, caffeine and cocaine especially, to keep themselves stimulated. They also tend to impose the brushfire management style on everyone below them.

Steve's specialty is the midnight meeting. Midnight meetings can be at 7 A.M., but Steve usually starts them with an urgent memo or phone call to all his managers to drop everything and be there at once. When the managers arrive, they find Steve standing, rubbing his hands and smiling as he says, "Well, the company's in big trouble today. Here's the problem." Then he states the latest threat to his company's existence.

At one meeting, he was waiting at the door with little baseball hats that said "Steve's SWAT team" for all the committee members. Steve was a bit hurt when people did not want to wear them.

His managers are ambivalent. They know the crises are important, but they also know that this is the way Steve does business. He likes to stir things up, and he has some success running his company this way. But his crisis-a-minute style is extremely hard on his employees who have day-to-day duties that need to get done, plus families and obligations outside work.

Steve lost some of his best people as soon as they matured enough to become really well-rounded managers. He's just as happy, though, to keep the younger, SWAT-team type, and it's his company, so he can do what he wants.

Stress-Related Problems

Dinosaur Brain managers tend to have problems with stress caused by over-arousal. They usually fit the criteria for Type A personality. In the early 1960s, when the Type A and B personalities were first defined, Type As were considered the bad guys and Type Bs the good guys. That was when people in my field were admonishing the world to lie back and take it easy, to go with the flow and the like. Now, as the importance of achievement is recognized, new studies are finding that Type As don't have quite as many heart attacks as they were thought to have, and they do tend to achieve more than Type Bs.

The current thinking is that impulsive types are at higher risk for heart attacks if they frequently have hostile feelings toward other people, a low tolerance for frustration and a tendency toward impatience and irritability. The more productive Type As, who have fewer heart attacks, tend to be more balanced, perhaps more intuitive, and maybe a little more mature.

The impulsive pattern, in moderation, is necessary for any professional achievement. Things just don't get moving without impulsiveness. Impulsive people make good entrepreneurs, but even entrepreneurs need to check the books occasionally and change course.

The hardest thing for these people to do is wait. If they have to wait, they'll often jump into rash action.

Paula was hired as a production assistant six months ago—actually, six months and ten days ago, she'll point out heatedly—and she still hasn't gotten a raise. She can't understand it, especially since Terry, who's only been here for four months, was just promoted to associate. Paula knows she has to do something and do it now. As soon as she takes three more aspirin to kill this splitting headache, she's going to march right into her boss's office and get some answers.

Regular exercise, a good diet, and refraining from overuse of stimulants and depressants are important in managing stress. That's the long-term approach. Impulsives want results quickly. Most of them are not drug abusers, but many get going with a few cups of coffee in the morning, then unwind with a few drinks in the evening. Over the long run, this leads to a depletion of certain chemicals and nutrients in the brain that makes the cortex less effective in its ability to inhibit the Dinosaur Brain, which leads to more impulsiveness and more stress. Most important, people who use this low-level drug plan don't get the chance to stimulate and relax themselves naturally. They rely on outside agents to do it for them.

Continued arousal wears out the body and mind prematurely. The people who succumb to stress-related disorders are people who tend to allow their Dinosaur Brains to control their lives.

Difficulties with Ethics

This is by no means true of all impulsive people, but for some adrenaline junkies the excitement of ill-gotten gains cannot be matched within the legal world. Ethical problems often are the result of the way the Dinosaur Brain operates.

Ethics of all kinds are based on balancing the needs of several different constituencies and deciding which is highest. When the Dinosaur Brain is in full tilt, that is just impossible. The Dinosaur Brain can focus on only one set of needs at a time. Sometimes that leads to decisions that have ethical implications.

Art has a division to run, and that division has to make a profit. The pressure is strong on him to have a good bottom line. Once, by accident, he double-billed on a government contract and it wasn't noticed. Here and there on subsequent billings, Art began to insert one or two little items— $87.50 for a hammer with a fancy name; $10 each for tenpenny nails; $180 for three nuts and bolts. He discovered that a lot of things could be buried in a complex billing. At first it was a way to ease the pressure, but later it became downright exciting. It became particularly exciting six years later, when the government decided to audit the contracts.

Are You Impulsive?

Everyone has impulsive tendencies, but most impulsive people don't tend to see themselves as such. They usually think they're smarter than other people but have more than their share of bad luck. They tend to have a hard time seeing where they fit into the big picture and especially how their actions affect other people.

How do you tell if you are impulsive? Some of the signs are:

> You often find your work boring and don't do certain required things regularly just because they're too dull.
>
> People have told you more than twice that you don't remember the promises you make.
>
> You have difficulty following through, or you don't listen to other people.
>
> You've had more than one or two instances where you've had to change a major decision because you didn't think of something that later turned out to be important.

The impulsive Dinosaur Brain really exhibits an immature or adolescent pattern. Our culture is very youth-oriented, and this style is extremely attractive to us. Impulsive people who have high energy and get things done are often forgiven much. Many have become heroes for taking impulsive action. Think of Daniel Boone, Davy Crockett, Billy the Kid, Andy Warhol, P.T. Barnum, George S. Patton, Oliver North and JFK, for that matter.

There is little in American folklore about maturity. If we compare American to Oriental heroes, we find that Oriental mythology has fewer gunfighters and more heroes who are men of wisdom, understanding and age, whose words seem opaque and require us to think about them before we understand them.

Usually people who are impulsive tend to grow out of it, but when they do is totally up to them. Some people can be teenagers well into their eighties.

So what do you do if you're a bit too impulsive?

1. *Learn to monitor your own arousal.* Listen to your heart. When people are aroused, their heart rate usually goes up. If you're a runner or into aerobics, you know what your resting pulse rate is. (The average for men is about 72; for women, about 78.) If you do that kind of exercise, you know how to take your pulse rate unobtrusively. For the more sedentary, if you are aware of your heart beating, then you probably need to sit down and relax. Be circumspect about the decisions you make when you are in that state. Other signs of heightened stress level include tension in neck muscles, headache, trembling, tightness in the chest or fidgeting.

2. *Recognize the warning signs of overload.* Certain kinds of behavior, thoughts and even dreams can indicate the Dinosaur Brain is too active. Usually they're behaviors that seem unusual or even a little bit weird to the people who find themselves acting this way. Typical warning signs can be forgetting things, making odd mistakes (putting your Filofax into the refrigerator, trying to lock your office with your car keys, humming disco music); or emotional and physical changes, such as headaches, upset stomach, food cravings or nightmares.

Know that your decisions may suffer when you are in a state of overload. See Chapter 18 for a more detailed guide to coping with stress and recognizing its different forms.

3. *Learn some relaxation techniques.* There are many on the market, including self-hypnosis, meditation, exercise, biofeedback, massage and martial arts. Anyone in business needs to be able to relax on demand and to know the difference between being relaxed and aroused. You must be able to lower your physiological responses when you need to, as soon as you notice your tension is up. For most people, just sitting down, taking a few deep breaths, clearing the head and agreeing not to take action until they feel calmer are all that it takes. A technique is presented in detail in Chapter 18.

4. *Master goal-oriented thinking.* In any situation at work, be able to stop and ask, What am I trying to do? What's my goal? Then check to see that your actions fit your goal. It's a good plan to make yourself aware of the competing goals in your life—with subordinates, professional competition, family—and understand the balancing that's required.

5. *Be aware of Dinosaur Brain patterns.* The more you learn, the more you'll recognize the specifics of the Dinosaur Brain in operation. In other words, if you suspect that you are an impulsive manager, you really ought to read the rest of this book, not just the one or two chapters that interest you right now.

6. *Give people you trust the right to comment on your behavior and decisions.* Impulsive people often tend to surround themselves with other impulsives, so that everybody is saying, "Yeah, yeah, great, let's do it." Accept the impulsive tendency in yourself and try to compensate for it by cultivating some relationships with people who are more circumspect and cautious. Let them tell you when your Dinosaur Brain is in control. Listen to what they say, and, at least half the time, modify your behavior based on what they've told you.

7. *Accept criticism as input.* Even when you're sure the criticism is personal, it's best not to act that way.

8. *Learn how to tolerate boredom.* Practice sitting around doing nothing or sticking with a boring task until it's done. Read nineteenth century novels instead of Robert Ludlum.

Working with Impulsives

If you work with impulsive people, deal with them gently. Tell them their strong points, and gently let them know their weak points. Give them assignments in which you can use their ideas and energy, especially as project-starters and crisis-solvers. Make sure they have one clear, overriding goal.

Don't put them where interpersonal relationships are the key issues. They are definitely not the people to "shape up" a troubled department; they'll only make matters worse. They are short-run people, who can make speeches and inspire, but they typically are not good at soothing damaged egos or mediating between two opposing factions.

Avoid attacks of any sort. Set ground rules for meetings or interactions. Use questioning creatively, not only as a way of getting information from them, but also as a chance to get them to stop and think or to clarify their priorities. (For instance, ask, What is most important to do? What can wait?)

Impulsive people tend to talk rapidly and make it hard for you to get a word in edgewise. If you want them to notice you, start out by speaking as loudly and quickly as they do. Then adjust your pacing to slower and softer. If you start out slow and soft, they'll just run right over you.

Finally, for your own sanity, learn to recognize when the Dinosaur Brains are in full control so you will know when to back off and leave them to their own mistakes.

4

The Triple F Response: Fight, Flight or Fright

For the briefest instant, frozen, the giants face each other warily, growling and drooling. Their tiny minds struggle with the one bit of free will nature allows: Fight or Run. There is no forgiveness in the dinosaur world. Those who make the wrong decision become lunch.

The wiring in the human nervous system is complex, involving connections not only with the brain, but also with the heart, glands, muscles and nearly every other part of the body. We feel many of the brain's responses in our bodies rather than hearing them inside our minds.

A subloop called the sympathetic nervous system is involved in virtually all Dinosaur Brain patterns. This system makes us immediately able to respond to threat with physical action. Sympathetic response is usually called Fight or Flight, but I call it the Fight, Flight or Fright Response, because sometimes it involves immobilization and overload.

When we're faced with a threat, our heart rate speeds up; breathing becomes rapid and shallow; we take in extra oxygen; muscles tense; the blood vessels near the surface of the skin contract, and blood is diverted to the muscles that will take the action. The adrenal glands keep pumping for all they're worth, and the mind becomes focused on simple, primitive patterns from the Dinosaur Brain: Fight back or run away.

When the focus moves from the cortex to the Dinosaur Brain, we can't really think any more. We can only react or become overloaded and blank out, immobilized.

Remember the last time you slammed on the brakes in the car to avoid hitting something? Your heart was pounding, and it probably took you five minutes to loosen your death-grip on the steering wheel. Your mind shut down, except for the image of that object in front of you and the physical reaction of going for the brakes.

That was the Triple F Response control. It saved you then, when you needed a fast physical reaction. You also encounter it every day at work, when the dangers you face usually aren't physical but are threats to your self-esteem. Problems arise when you try to protect your psyche with defensive systems that were designed to protect your body. Dinosaurs, after all, didn't have to worry about self-esteem.

The Dinosaur Brain tends to see the world in terms of potential threats. During a typical day at the office, anything that might cause us to look bad to ourselves or others can set off our threat alarms. Our Dinosaur Brains have made up rules to protect us from ridicule and dangers to self-esteem. Some of those rules might be:

Be perfect!
Be wary. People are out to get you!
Don't trust anyone in authority!
Never admit you're wrong!
Get even!
Defend yourself!
Cover your tail!

Sometimes the rules would sound pretty flaky if we talked about them, but we don't talk about them; we just act on them.

Charlotte knows her boss doesn't like her. He has made critical comments and changed some of her duties. When he gave her a "needs improvement" rating on interpersonal skills, she felt it was time to stand up for herself. She went right upstairs to the vice-president and told him about her unfair treatment. She also wrote a memo protesting her performance evaluation and is now recording her boss's every move in writing.

Charlotte's defensive actions led to just the result she feared most. They made her boss even more angry at her, and he began cracking down even harder. Of course, she felt that he was just showing his true colors and that she had to defend herself even more.

It's impossible to convince Charlotte that she has any responsibility in this conflict. Inside her head, she runs over and over a list of all the things her boss has done to her. Every time she replays the list, she gets more and more irritated, upset and frightened.

This story illustrates one of the ways the Dinosaur Brain works. Charlotte used her Dinosaur Brain; her boss responded to her Lizard Logic. Then Charlotte, seeing her dinosaur perceptions confirmed, became even more aroused. Adrenal glands pumping, heart beating, all systems on red-alert, her body was ready to take action, and her actions did nothing to enhance her career.

The good thing about the Dinosaur Brain is that, once the conflict is over, it's done and forgotten. Yet there's another problem with the Triple F Response, which comes with the addition of the cortex. Your brain is a very complex information-processing system and has one big, glaring defect. Overall, it cannot tell reality from fantasy. To use the technical psychological term, your brain is crazy.

The human mind is predisposed to deal with unfinished situations. This is good for survival, because we have to be able to pick up on what we were doing if we're distracted. The trouble is that inter-personal relationships are never finished until we say they are.

Most of us run a negative situation over and over in our minds, trying to gain closure on it. Instead, we usually arouse ourselves more and make the situation more important. The more we think about a negative situation, the more important it becomes. With each retelling inside our heads, we change the details a little bit more to conform to our preconceptions of the world. Goethe said that when pride and memory quarrel, pride always wins. This ruminating makes us more sure that the world is as we think it is; we act on it; our actions cause more problems with stress.

Let's say you get into a confrontation with your boss. Not only do you have to deal with your Dinosaur Brain response while the conflict is happening, but your cortex is also worrying about it before it occurs and rehashing it afterward. Since your brain can't tell whether what's going on is real or fantasy, you get the same physiological reaction. Your system can stay aroused around the clock, which is why job stress is such a big problem. You can leave the work at the office, but sometimes mentally you can't leave the situation that causes your arousal. You have the stress, the wear and tear of the Triple F Response, not only when the confrontation is happening, but also at breakfast that morning, in the car on the way home, at night as you watch television, and after midnight when you can't fall asleep. Your mind's internal television keeps playing some of its scariest programs.

In Chapter 18 we see how to use this defect in the central nervous system to actually lower your arousal. We also look at ways to make stress less stressful. Now let's consider the three Dinosaur Brain defensive patterns. We all use the three responses to different degrees, but some people have a particular style that relies on one of the three.

Fight

Fight people are competitive, even at things that don't matter. Whatever they're doing, they want to win. Even if they're playing games with their children, it's difficult for them to lose. These people would rather be right than happy.

They're also always under time pressure. They have the Dinosaur Brain's impulsive pattern, and they deal angrily with any kind of frustration or delay. If something gets in their way or blocks them from their immediate goal, they will get mad at it, yell at it or try to bite its head off.

Fighters are usually overly sensitive to anything that might be a threat. Everything is personal; everything is on the record. On every issue, no matter how small, there is a winner and a loser; you can be sure that a fighter is not going to be the loser.

It's almost constitutionally impossible for these people to let a slight go by. They expect that other people will frustrate or fight them and, as we have seen, this often causes exactly what they expect.

Fighters expect that everyone else is playing by their rules too. You're likely to hear them say, "It's a dog-eat-dog world out there," or "Fight fire with fire." They tend to be abrasive and to attack anyone who criticizes them.

Yet abrasive people often don't see themselves as such, maybe because nobody has ever told them they are. (Of course they haven't—they're afraid of being yelled at.) As I read Lee Iaccoca's autobiography, it seemed to me that he is an extremely abrasive person. It's interesting that he says so little about the effect of his abrasiveness on other people. Then again, would *you* tell Lee Iaccoca he was abrasive?

Fight people are very similar to the hostile Type As, the people who are at risk for heart attacks. It is not within the scope of this book to look at the Type A and B dichotomy, but if this applies to you, you might want to look into the health problems linked to hostility and aggressiveness.

If your Dinosaur Brain is always screaming, "Fight, fight, fight!" recognize this tendency in yourself and learn to use it selectively.

1. Always ask yourself, "What do I win if I compete in this situation, and is what I would win important to me? Is it important enough to risk the animosity of the person I'm competing with?" Know that it's you who's a hostile person, not that it's a hostile world.

2. Be able to monitor your own arousal level. When your heart is pounding, your neck is tense, your breathing is short and sharp,

and your hands are clenched into fists, make sure you keep your mouth shut. Very little that you say in situations like that will be helpful. Go to another room, work on something else. Cool down. It helps to know a technique for physically relaxing. One of the many available methods will be discussed in Chapter 18.

3. Pay attention to your internal chatter. Be alert to Dinosaur Brain lines, such as "I can't believe this . . . ," "I've told him a million times . . . ," and "If that doesn't beat everything. . . ." When these shows are playing on your internal television, change the channel.

4. Force yourself to let other people win. Use your cortex: Gaining allies might be a more effective strategy than beating out everybody. Dinosaurs didn't need allies, but you probably do.

5. As simple as it sounds, force yourself to smile and say nice things to people. All animals have innate signs that their intent is not hostile. For humans, smiling and extending an open hand are the main ones. A smile is incompatible with aggression. (Yes, I know about irony. You can feel really hostile and smile at the same time, but in general, the more you smile and say nice things to people, the less angry you'll feel. Try it; you'll see.)

6. Try to develop the attitude that J.D. Salinger calls reverse paranoia. One of his fictional characters says, "I consider myself a reverse paranoiac. I am always suspecting that people might be conspiring to make me happy." That is about as clear and concise a definition of mental health as I can imagine.

Flight

This part of the Triple F Response deals with avoidance, which can take many forms, including procrastination, forgetting, running away and being sick. Flight always involves choosing the easier of two paths, even when you know the harder one is better for you. The usual approach is indecisiveness.

Arthur is bright; everybody knows that, and he knows it, too. He could do more than be a production supervisor. He has talked about getting another job or having more responsibility, and he has even been able to land some promotions within the company. Usually about two days before the new job is supposed to start, Arthur turns it down because he knows he just won't be able to perform well enough. He even quit a job after holding it for a week and asked for his old job back. He said he just couldn't hack the pressure and asked, "What do I need with a job that's stressful? I'm not ambitious."

Yet Arthur keeps thinking about other jobs he might have and ways that he could develop his potential. Everybody else knows that he will retire from the job he's in.

Many people have a delusion that life presents them with a right choice and a wrong one, and that they should be able to tell which is which in advance. More often, in this ambiguous world, we have to choose something and, by our commitment to it, make it the right choice. Either option can be correct if we're willing to make it so. What causes the problem is never making a decision or jumping from one choice to another without a clear focus on our action.

Another common pattern involves being just too busy to do what you're afraid of doing. Impulsive people are good at this. Their Dinosaur Brains are always pointing out new emergencies that make them too busy to do the more important work, which also happens to be the most difficult and threatening.

Whenever you ask Deb how she's doing, it's, "Busy, busy, busy. Got to run." She always has something going on and, if you glanced at her, it would seem she was accomplishing quite a bit. Deb is really doing a lot of little errands, all easy and nonthreatening. The big sales report that's due at the end of the quarter is sitting under a stack of her phone messages. She will probably get a deadline extension because she was just too busy to finish it on time.

Deb's real problem is that everything else took priority over the difficult and challenging report. This is why time management is a problem for so many people. It isn't too hard to manage time itself; time is very predictable. There's no way to turn a day into 25 hours. The real problem is priorities.

The Dinosaur Brain is always telling you to do the easiest and least frightening stuff first, or to jump in and handle whatever is making the most noise. The secret to managing time is learning how to recognize and manage your Dinosaur Brain.

Another avoidance technique is assuming that it's impossible for you to act, because everything is under somebody else's control.

Mark knows what it takes to sell real estate, but the market is very soft now. Interest rates are fluctuating wildly, and the area still hasn't fully recovered from the recession. Not only that, but it all depends on who you know, and Mark is just getting started. These are the things that he thinks about while he sits in his office, waiting for somebody to call.

What do you do if you're an avoider? The answer is simple, but you won't like it. You have to set priorities and stick to them. If there is a hard way and an easy way, take the hard way, because with your style, you can usually be sure that the hard way is right for you.

When your Dinosaur Brain says that a particular choice is the right one, and you know that choice is easiest, say, "Get thee behind me, Satan," and ignore it.

Practice making decisions and sticking to them, no matter what, for a period of time. I am talking long periods, like six months to a year. The Dinosaur Brain needs to know that your cortex's decisions are important and will stand. Start out with little choices and move on to bigger ones.

Fright

What we are talking about here is blanking out and becoming immobilized, being unable to act, or restricting your actions because you're afraid. This is probably the most serious of the three Triple F patterns because it involves a stimulation overload, similar to what a power surge does to your computer. Your arousal level becomes so high that you actually act like a dinosaur. You might physically get up and run out of the room or send your mind out while you remain, trembling.

If you have this pattern to any great extent, you might need professional help. This section is not designed to deal with a full-blown phobia, but rather to cope with certain situations that are so frightening that they can cause you to blank out occasionally.

The most widespread example of the fright response is the fear of public speaking, including cold calls.

Edna just can't speak in public. Her mind goes blank, and she can't think of what to say. Her boss knows this, so if somebody in the department has to do a presentation, it certainly won't be Edna. The boss is a good manager, and she tries to use people for their best talents, so Edna gets to do the work behind the scenes. Her boss doesn't realize that she is rewarding Edna for being afraid of public speaking.

What should Edna do? Here are some general guidelines.

1. Most important, don't use fear as an excuse for avoiding anything. If you are afraid of something, force yourself to approach it. It will be scary at first, but the more you practice, the easier it will become. Recognize your internal voice trying to talk you into running away. Talk back.

2. Learn a relaxation technique. Use it. Practice, practice, practice.

3. Restructure the threatening situation so that it is not so alien. The more you say, "I can't," the more it becomes true. Look instead for what you *can* do within the situation and build on that.

There's an "up" side to two of the three elements in the Triple F Response: They can keep you out of trouble. Fight can be channeled to improve motivation and protect you from people who might take advantage of you. Flight can let you know when to stop pushing. Fright, though, is seldom good for anything. All of the elements of fright, if untempered by the cortex, will lead to stress and misery.

5

Be Dominant!

All eyes are on the old bull. First in everything, he gets his choice: food, females, whatever life has to offer, but he pays a price in dedication and vigilance.

A young male approaches with teeth bared and a growl beginning deep in his throat. The challenger has trained for this day by taking on and defeating other powerful young bulls. He bears his scars, but he's ready. The battle is on. To the winner, power. To the loser, death or exile. There can only be one chairman of the board.

The Dinosaur Brain believes:

1. There is only one pecking order, and you have to be tough, competitive and aggressive to move up in it.

2. Business is red in fang and claw. If people fall along the way, it is evidence that they didn't have what it takes to survive. Their loss is of no consequence.

3. The only rule is "The strong survive."

4. Every conflict is a struggle for power. No area is too small. The dominant lizard is first in everything.

5. Dominant dinosaurs not only run the show, they *own* the show. They make rules for the underlings, but they stand above the law.

The cortex thinks:

1. Blind aggressiveness is not the only game in town.

2. Unbridled, aggressive competitiveness within the company is expensive in terms of alienation, distrust and wasted effort. It's often hard to look out only for yourself *and* for the company.

3. The aggression and anger involved in perpetual struggles for dominance cause needless wear and tear on the company and the individual.

The corporate world sends mixed signals on the aggressive pursuit of dominance. Is competition the only way to the top, or is team playing rewarded? Companies differ in their philosophy; writers differ in their approach. There are no easy answers and recommendations.

Input and the sharing of power are fine, but you can't run a corporation by vote. Certain people, whether by election, appointment or corporate combat, must be at the top to make decisions that affect everyone else.

What we call "personal ambition" is really striving for dominance. It comes from the Dinosaur Brain. Without the drive to get to the top, the whole corporate structure would fall. The Dinosaur Brain's problem lies in believing that the only way to the top is through competition within the company. I call this the zero-sum fallacy: the belief that if someone wins, someone else has to lose. A number of companies are examining their values regarding internal competition and cooperation.

Status versus Leadership

An early Paul Klee etching is called *Two Men Meet, Each Supposing the Other Is of Higher Rank.* The two are bowing, and each is watching to see how low the other bows. This is a graphic example of what goes on in a dominance conflict.

When you get involved in a power play, other things seem to recede. It's hard to think about anything but who's on top. Some management authorities have promoted this kind of Dinosaur Brain self-indulgence with books about getting ahead through clever manipulation and the notion of Power: power talking, power lunches, power walk, power stance, even power ties. The theory behind it is very simple: If you act dominant, you will be seen as dominant. People will defer to you and probably promote you.

There is a problem with this approach. The prescription for dominance says that power involves acting or looking as much as possible like a tall, wealthy, Eastern male. Obviously, some people are more convincing than others.

I have seen graduates of power classes who don't bring off the program very well. Once, at a meeting, I noticed a young executive scowling in a peculiar way. He looked a lot like Snoopy from "Peanuts," sitting on his doghouse, pretending to be a vulture. After the meeting I asked what he was doing. He admitted he was practicing his power look.

The way to deal with power-hungry lizards is absurdly simple: Don't engage them in a dominance fight. Let them talk louder, interrupt or sit at the commanding place at the table. Let them look their power looks. Just realize what is going on and don't give in to them on issues that you think are important. In most cases you can win by not fighting: Squabbling dinosaurs don't inspire too much credibility. Their Dinosaur Brains expect that if you accede in one area, you'll give in on others. That doesn't have to be the case. Let them prance and posture all they want while you enjoy the show. You must, however, be able to be assertive on the important points and know when to speak up and how to make yourself heard.

There's no doubt that Charley wants to move up in the company, but so does everybody else. It's just that Charley's way of doing it is so different. On the surface, it seems that he is doing everything all wrong. It starts with his tweed jacket in a gray pinstripe world.

While the other middle managers are always trying to demonstrate their intelligence and play up their own ideas, Charley acts like a team player. He always includes other people in his projects and really makes an effort to make them look good. He's the kind of guy who goes around the room and asks everybody else for an opinion, instead of shouting them down and hogging the spotlight. When somebody comes up with a creative suggestion, Charley's the first one to say, "Way to go!"

He doesn't gossip or form alliances; he seems to get along with everybody. All the up-and-coming guys like to work with Charley because he's always so willing to share the credit. Secretly a lot of them think he's pretty dumb for not promoting himself more than he does.

When the vice-president's slot opened, everybody was surprised when good old Charley was chosen—everybody except Charley. To salve their feelings, people said that he was a compromise candidate because the guys upstairs couldn't choose between two of the flashier young warriors. Charley knew different. He really understood the rules of dominance.

While the others were acting like people vying for a leadership role, Charley was acting like a leader. Nobody saw him as a particular threat. The people upstairs saw him as a team player, an organizer and a manager who could get the job done without getting too involved in time-consuming office politics.

Even though Charley was about the same age as everyone else, he purposely acted older and more mature. In the herd, the young warriors are always in competition among themselves. Instead of being seen as bright, flashy and aggressive, Charley concentrated on acting like a level-headed old bull. It worked.

Charley's good-guy approach was rewarded in the corporation that employed him, but in some other companies his actions would have branded him as a perpetual second banana. To get to the top he eventually would have had to turn aggressive. How would Charley fare in your company? See who gets promoted and structure your actions accordingly.

Corporate Style

Companies differ not only in their idea of how to get to the top, but also of what it means to be at the top. Corporate traditions and values are passed on very rapidly throughout a company by apocryphal stories that neatly sum up people's perceptions of the corporate style and other important abstract issues. Management's philosophy is usually passed on by some variation of the security guard story:

A new security guard sits at the desk in the main lobby of corporate headquarters. His job is to turn away everyone who's not wearing an identification badge. One day the chairman of the board, in shirt sleeves, walks through the door and heads for the staff entrance. The security guard stops him and prevents him from going upstairs until he is properly identified.

Is the guard fired or rewarded?

If he gets fired, this story contains the warning that some people function above the company rules, and if you try to enforce the rules on these king lizards, you're going to be in big trouble. If the security guard gets promoted or rewarded, that clearly says that the rules are for everyone.

If you aren't comfortable within a highly competitive corporate hierarchy, you may have an option other than leaving the company. Most businesses have departments—personnel, public relations, law, information systems—that aren't really part of the corporate hierarchy. They cost money and don't produce money. The work here is often more enjoyable because there's less pressure. You might consider a transfer to one of these.

If the crunch comes, however, the cuts come here first because these departments are usually not considered the "real" company. (Sometimes the department heads are considered part of the hierarchy, but usually no one else.) Beware of a move to one of these departments if you want to move up. Companies often get rid of women by promoting them to a more important job in a less important department, so that the sum total is a demotion.

Playing to Win

Unbridled competitiveness is destructive. The Dinosaur Brain is programmed so that, when the hierarchy is unclear, people will struggle
for dominance. In some corporations, this internecine struggle is
considered good management training, in fact, the only training
that's relevant. In others, it's not in the best taste.

*Peter is Mr. Competitiveness. His motto is, "If you're going to play at all,
you might as well win." No issue is too small. He advocates fiscal conservatism and keeps everybody on a short leash. His eye is always on this
quarter's bottom line. If it looks bad, he cuts expenses unmercifully.*

*In meetings Peter delights in making other people look stupid, and he always
has the last word. He speaks almost entirely in sports metaphors and quasi-
military slang. He likes talking about sending people a message, which
means clobber them to show them who's boss. (Speaking of boss, when his
is around, Peter becomes remarkably kind and solicitous. The term "brownnosing" might be a charitable description of his behavior.)*

Peter wins a lot of battles, but he is losing a war. His staff doesn't
trust him; they aren't loyal to him; they know they're all replaceable
so they watch out for themselves. His peers see him as someone
who would stab them in the back if somebody handed him a sharp
paper clip.

His rise in his first company was rapid, but suddenly he stopped
being promoted. He read the writing on the wall and found a job
with a different company, where his job history was repeated. Try
as he might—and he tried his damnedest—he always came in second.

Peter was the very essence of a lizard vying for dominance and
winning. What he didn't realize is that, in the lizard world, you kill
your rivals, but among humans, the people you step on often stay
around and can get you back. One of them singly may not be strong
enough to beat you, but when a few of them get together there can
be safety in numbers. If you don't believe me, just ask Julius Caesar.

Peter was dominant everywhere but a leader nowhere. Once you
are in a leadership role, you have to lead. In the herd only one leads

and all the rest follow; there is no middle management in the dinosaur world. For humans, you can compete with your peers to be a follower to those above you, but you have to lead your subordinates. Peter left out the "leader" part of the leadership role he so coveted.

Now let's take a look at how the Dinosaur Brain's appetite for dominance can be channeled effectively. Even a highly competitive person in a highly competitive setting does not have to be destructive.

Anne is bright and aggressive and wants to move up. Like most competitive people, she would like to win at everything, but she knows some games count more than others. She keeps her urge to win in check until she has thought through the situation and is sure that it will be to her benefit to win. When she fights, heads roll. She never draws her gun unless she intends to kill somebody.

If Anne is not at war with somebody, she is a loyal and true friend. She has thoroughly researched the qualities that her company values: a good bottom line, a smooth-running operation, loyalty from subordinates, new ideas that aren't too radical, and a bit of deference to those above.

When another manager made a dumb mistake, instead of blowing the whistle on him, Anne decided to spend a lot of her own time helping him out of the mess because she thought in the long run his loyalty would be better than his animosity.

In a meeting, another manager implied that Anne's department wasn't particularly efficient. She quietly stood up and said, "You may have a point there. I'm willing to accept your challenge. Why don't we set criteria and just see who runs a better operation for a year? Let's figure out how we are going to measure it."

That was a battle she had to win and she won it. Anne could use her Dinosaur Brain to motivate herself, but she didn't let it set her goals for her. She set the goals and made her efforts count. Her Dinosaur Brain was her powerful ally, but her cortex was always in control.

In most companies, Anne's style would be rewarded, although there are a few in which you have to be like Peter to get ahead. To decide on your own actions, gauge the political climate by the stories you hear and the behaviors of upper management you observe. Then balance that with your own comfort level.

To come out on top in long-term struggles for dominance, it takes a dinosaur with a cortex to channel destructive aggression into constructive self-promotion.

6

Defend the Territory!

An armor-plated, three-horned creature grazes in the sun. He placidly marks his area with droppings the size of cantaloupes. The land is his. What grows on it is his. The air over it is his. If anybody wants to dispute his claim, he'll be only too happy to comply. Go ahead, he snorts. Make my day.

When people behave in a territorial way, they look comical to other people and even feel funny to themselves, but they don't stop. Territoriality is serious. It's programmed so deeply inside that, to succeed in business, we have to live by it and understand it.

Let's look first at territoriality in its simplest form. Consider your desk. How would you feel if you walked in to work one morning and found that the stuff on the top of your desk had been moved around? Even worse, how would you react if you ushered a couple of people into your office for a meeting and one of them took your desk chair for his seat?

You'd be in a very tough bind. A part of you would be saying inside, "That's my chair! He has no right to do that!" and another part of you would reason, "Don't be silly. It's just a chair."

The agitation you'd feel in that situation is powerful and irrational and comes directly from the Dinosaur Brain. We're programmed to consider certain spaces as our own. We mark them with our possessions, like the pictures and calendars on our office walls, or the recliner at home and its nearby stack of territorial markers—*The Wall Street Journal*s and *Business Week*s—that show everyone that that's your space. How about the pink flamingos on your lawn? Correct: territorial droppings.

Names are very important too. The Dinosaur Brain makes no distinction between the name of the object and the object itself. Consider your job title and how it feels if somebody gets it wrong. Or maybe someone calls your car gray, when its actual color is "Black Forest smoke." If anybody intrudes on your territory, you feel attacked. This is not rational, but it's strong. We feel silly when we do it, but we do it just the same.

Territory and Personal Space

Territoriality also extends to the bubble of space we occupy. You know how uncomfortable it is when people stand too close; they have to be invited in or stay back at least two and a half feet. The amount of space required is cultural. Americans and the British tend to require more space than other cultures and are least comfortable standing close to others or touching.

In some Arab countries, there's a saying that if you trust a man, you should give him your breath. If you were thinking, "Yuck!" when you read that, you'll understand how emotional the issues of space and territory are.

Invading someone's personal space can be a device to maintain dominance in a situation. When it happens to you, you usually know something's going on, but it's often difficult to talk about a Dinosaur Brain issue like this.

Some people habitually stand too close or touch too much as a way of controlling you by keeping you off balance. If you begin backing up, you're seen as submissive. It's uncomfortable to talk to these people; often it's hard to put your finger on just what's bothering you. We usually don't talk or think about how close a person stands or how much he or she touches us; it sounds silly. (This doesn't mean you can't ever do it; sometimes it's appropriate.) Most often these pushy people are acting unconsciously, following the urges of their own Dinosaur Brains. If you talk to them about what they're doing, they may deny it.

To prevent the worst abuses, it's best to arrange to talk to these types of dinosaurs sitting down. You can also play the same game and let them back up; you'll be communicating directly to their Dinosaur Brains. (It's only breath.) Moving in on the personal space of an angry person is not such a good idea, however. It will be perceived as a threat.

Likewise, if somebody takes your chair as a device for keeping you off balance in a negotiation, you must be aware of it and use your cortex to recognize what's going on and keep yourself calm. You can't just suddenly stop negotiating the $10-million contract and do a scenario out of the Three Bears: "Somebody's sitting in MY chair!" Instead you should quietly choose another seat and remain focused on the contract—not on Goldilocks.

The most obvious connection between territory and dominance is size. The larger your office, desk or body, the more powerful you seem. Many books can teach you to use the concept of territory and dominance to win out in the dinosaur-eat-dinosaur world of business. For instance, one strategy is having people come to your office or desk for meetings or negotiations, because you are more powerful in your own territory than the person who has to come to you. However, it is the intention of this book to teach you how to use the Dinosaur Brain concept to avoid needless conflict rather than to perpetuate conflict or exploit others.

For our purposes, the most important aspect of territoriality is the perception from the outside that it's silly, when it is really anything but silly. For example, take a look at jurisdictional disputes among unions. Outsiders often look at them and say, "Those guys always fight about the silliest little issues," but to the people involved in the dispute, jurisdiction is a life-and-death issue. It has to do with more than money; it means defending the territory for survival.

Territory in today's business world is defined less by space and more in terms of function, budget and information. All territoriality, however, seems to follow the rules for land: There's a limited amount; all of it is taken; and if young dinosaurs want any territory, they have to take it from others who already have it. Sometimes the results of these land grabs can be very detrimental, not only to the young turks' careers but also to the company.

Territoriality is also what makes it so hard for executives to delegate successfully. Delegation is like giving away land; it means giving somebody something to do that you wouldn't mind doing yourself, as well as the authority to do it. Executives need to delegate authority or they become overwhelmed, but many of them get caught up in the idea of owning and doing it all themselves. This is what I refer to as "the Captain Kirk management style" in Chapter 23.

When our territory is threatened, it seems to be more valuable to us. Often during rough times in business, people blindly hold on to jobs they should have moved out of long ago, simply because they are threatened. Many competent people seem to have the delusion that the jobs they're in are the only jobs they can ever have. They nearly have to be kicked out before they'll look for a new position, even if a different job might be a better use of their talents.

If you wake up in the middle of the night, thinking, "What will happen to me if I lose my job?" that can be a good sign that you ought to consider quitting. When a job becomes your property, it becomes ritualistic and stultified. It's usually not good for you or your company, particularly if you really want a career rather than a job.

Territoriality can also be positive; it can lead to esprit de corps. People need to feel that their jobs are important and require special skills, that not just anybody can do them. Think of the Marine Corps' slogan, "We're looking for *a few* good men." These feelings of affiliation and loyalty, which arise from the Dinosaur Brain, are essential for motivation, as we discuss in Chapter 17.

How to Deal with Territoriality

The best way to cope with territoriality is to go along with it and consider it a necessary evil, because it can cause real trouble if you don't take it seriously.

Natalie is in charge of the data analysis department. In her little empire, she has rules about who comes in and how information is requested (usually in a memo in triplicate, addressed only to her).

Karen needs something done really quickly and, since she has a good relationship with one of the people in Natalie's department, she decides to go to that person directly and ask for what she needs.

When Natalie finds out what Karen has done, she is likely to raise a fuss, stop her request or, most likely, make it especially tough for Karen to get any information from her department ever again.

How do you deal with someone like this who defends her territory so fiercely?

1. *Stop.* Back up. Leave the territory and speak from the figurative boundary line. Once you are inside the territory, the lizard will be too agitated to try to do anything except drive you out. Instead, communicate from the border. Use the channels that the lizard has decreed are appropriate. Write a memo, make a phone call, set up a meeting, whatever is the proper way to gain access to her territory. If you try to sneak in the back door, you might accomplish your immediate goal of getting something done, but the lizard will be much more difficult to deal with in the long run.

2. *Validate the lizard's position as owner of the territory.* Often a good way to do this is using the person's title. "You're head of data processing, Natalie, after all, and I need your help."

3. *Most of all, don't laugh.* Take it seriously. Remember that territory is survival.

Herb is the company's computer wizard. Everybody knows he's the only one who can understand all the complicated new software. If somebody needs computer data, Herb's the man to ask. He's always so good-natured about filling requests that hardly anybody complains about how long it takes to get the information. But Herb grew quite red-faced and huffy when several of the department managers started messing around with the system and discovered that it really wasn't as mysterious as Herb had led them to believe. When one of them asked for access to programming information, Herb warned him that he didn't really understand what he was doing. And everybody knows that a little knowledge is a dangerous thing.

Herb's Dinosaur Brain defined computers as his territory. If everybody understood them, then he lost ground. Never mind what's best for the company. His Dinosaur Brain perceived the managers' interest as a threat, and Herb fought against it by getting angry and using what sounded like a logical argument.

He has maneuvered himself into the dangerous position of standing against progress. His Dinosaur Brain tells him it's the only way to survive. His cortex could tell him he could gain stature and authority by offering to oversee a company-wide software training program, but he probably won't think of it.

Territorial behaviors look petty and insignificant to others, which often leads people not to take them seriously and, maybe, to poke and prod the boundaries. This perception isn't rational either, and, like territoriality itself, it comes from the Dinosaur Brain.

We're all imperialists sometimes; we have the innate urge to try the limits of other people's territories and, if they don't defend themselves, their territory becomes our own. This is why there are so many turf struggles at work. They're going to happen, so you should know the rules. Later, this chapter discusses how to prevent them.

A good empire-builder can win many of these struggles over the years and gain a powerful hold over certain functions within the company. Usually the strategy involves having control over expenditure or information and, only occasionally, space.

At first the consolidation of power is efficient, and the empire-builder is applauded. If the empire gets larger and the emperor grows older, his territory can become a small barony within the company, with its own goals that may not be consistent with the company's overall objectives.

An empire-builder's chief goal is to hold on to power. When an empire becomes too large, it not only can stand in the way of productivity, it can also get in the way of people's careers. An emperor can cause channels to move so slowly and control so many different areas that people gradually realize that, if they are to move up, the empire must fall, which breeds aggression and counteraggression.

Many productive careers could be ruined on the battlefield of a turf struggle, but what can you do with an old dinosaur emperor who has outlived his usefulness? Most upper management would be reluctant to take away any of his functions because he hasn't really done anything to deserve this loss of face, at least from upper management's viewpoint. What actually happens is that the emperor is brought down by young contenders who are vying for their own territories.

Purchasing is the heart of darkness at the center of Lizardbrain, Inc. The purchasing manager, Mr. Kurtz, has been there as long as anybody remembers and runs his own little empire. To get anything, whether it's a desktop computer, a company car or paper clips, you have to request from purchasing. How and when your request will be acted on depends on how Kurtz views you or your department.

Kurtz signs off on everything; nobody makes a single decision without his approval. His top managers have adopted his style too. The upshot is that purchasing is a powerful little kingdom within the company, operating with its own rules and for its own benefit.

Kurtz regards every penny of the company's money as if it were his own. He tries to set up barriers against spending, and he keeps a list of foolish requests that he uses to humiliate sinners and to demonstrate that, unless he were watchful, the company would go to hell in a handbasket. Even people who don't like him have to admit that he knows his job. It seems he has hundreds of inventories, catalogs and price lists inside his head.

Upper management used to adore Kurtz because he kept costs down and maintained excellent records. Only in the last few years has the CEO begun to realize how much Kurtz's "efficiency" costs. People often go weeks and weeks without basic supplies, which is costing the company a lot in time and making-do, not to mention morale.

There is a question whether Kurtz is good or bad for the company. If the corporation is finance-driven, he is definitely good. Over the years, however, he has become more conservative and behind the times; less of a watchdog and more of a dog in the manger. Kurtz's hit-list is legendary, as is his skill at back-biting and bad-mouthing certain people who annoy him.

Upper management had begun to see Kurtz as a problem but was unwilling to step in and change the function of so powerful a department. Its decision was to step back and allow lower-level people to try to take him on. This kind of malignant strategy is often called "benign neglect."

Gayle, a new manager in a smaller department, took a shot at bringing him down, but her complaints about his pettiness and mean-spiritedness fell on deaf ears. She had no support base of her own matched against Kurtz's entrenched empire. Gayle got clobbered.

Ted tried to go around him by buying some things from petty cash or trying to bury requests for basic equipment within other lengthy budgets. Kurtz, however, could always find the buried treasures and would pronounce them expensive and wasteful. Ted struck out too.

Kurtz was the corporate jungle incarnate, but by now, even the jungle wanted him dead. Jeff finally broke his stranglehold. Jeff never took Kurtz on directly. In fact, he filled out his paperwork impeccably and never missed a chance to compliment Kurtz publicly. In fact, Jeff followed many of the behaviors recommended for dealing successfully with the Kurtzes of this world: Don't let them bother you and do things their way.

But Jeff was after Kurtz's head. He knew that, if he could figure out some way for the company to authorize equipment purchases without going through Kurtz, Kurtz's hold would be broken.

After much research in management journals, Jeff came up with the idea of the "experimental" project budget. This plan gave a project manager a total sum to complete his or her project, including purchasing equipment.

Kurtz protested, saying the idea was wasteful and inefficient. Who else could ever have access to all the price-related information that he had, already stored in his memory? Jeff agreed and suggested that Kurtz set the project budget himself.

Of course, Kurtz's figure was bare bones, as Jeff had known it would be, but Jeff was willing to take it on. He knew that coming in under the line would break Kurtz's hold and give the departments a new system for ordering their equipment. If, however, he asked for one penny extra, Kurtz's old system would win.

Jeff never told anyone about his hidden agenda. He was a real slave driver on the project, but when it came in three thousand dollars below budget, he knew he had won. It wasn't long before the project budget model was being used all over the company.

Kurtz's retirement party was the biggest bash Lizardbrain, Inc. had ever seen and, for once, no expense was spared.

The foregoing is a tragedy in the classical sense. Empires carry the seeds of their own destruction. The secret is that they are vulnerable only to their own rules. Should you be contemplating overthrowing an empire, you must know the empire's rules. A system set up to save money must be shown to be wasteful. (Jeff demonstrated that purchasing was an unnecessary middleman.) A system to ensure efficiency must be shown to be inefficient. It will take hard work and facts to back up all contentions. May the force be with you.

The other problem with empires is that they seldom last into the next generation. If you don't believe me, consider the experiences of Charlemagne or King Lear.

How Management Can Avoid Empire-Building

Companies must come to grips with territoriality. The best time for management to deal with it is before it becomes a major source of conflict. Here's how:

1. *Take people's territorial feelings seriously.* Realize that employees feel as if they own their jobs. If you change their duties, take away professional privileges or otherwise move things around, they will feel as if you're taking away a part of themselves.

2. *Realize you can make territoriality work for or against the company.* It must be planned; if you don't plan for it, the turf issues will grow up on their own. Turf struggles are the norm rather than anomalies.

It must be clear who has control over what, or people will fight over virtually anything. Resist the temptation to say, "Work it out among yourselves," because that is siding with the most aggressive. This may not be the precedent you want to set.

There is a thin line between giving people authority over their own jobs and setting the conditions for establishing empires. The only people who really can draw that line are the CEO and maybe the board of directors, most of whom, by the way, probably reached their positions through a consolidation of power.

3. *Determine department size by need.* In many companies, managerial status is judged by department size. The rationale that size equals status provides incentive for adding functions and people who really don't belong there.

In the best of all possible worlds, the company would organize job functions according to who needs to do what to accomplish specific goals. This practice would be monitored and accepted company-wide. The overall corporate welfare would come before anyone's personal feelings. Compensation and promotion would be based on accomplishment instead of how many resources or people a manager controls. As you can see, this would be difficult for many companies.

4. *Look for empires in your own company.* You may discover them by tracing a couple of new projects from idea to implementation. You might find that certain flow charts always seem to route themselves through certain offices, and new projects sometimes seem to choose certain desks on which to die.

If you find that you have the beginnings of an empire, you need to meet with the emperor-apparent and possibly buy back certain of his or her functions for the common good. You might give the person a raise or new quarters or some other face-saving symbol of power in return for removing responsibilities.

If you simply take functions away, the person will be angry and will probably feel demoted or want to retaliate. Sometimes the only thing you can do is get rid of an empire by stripping the emperor of power and control, but in other cases, a deal can be worked out.

5. *Employ a customer service model.* The model described in Chapter 16 can do a lot to get around some of the thornier and more difficult

issues involved in territoriality and dominance by making departments more answerable to one another. The solutions, as always,
lie in using the cortex to make the best out of what's in the Dinosaur
Brain.

7

Get the Mate!

The season comes to a distant rain forest; the giant dinosaur seeks a mate. He preens, puffs and parades before the females until he finds one who is receptive. He singles her out from the herd, and they begin the intricate dance of courtship. Their tiny brains shut out all thoughts except of each other and of what comes next.

He approaches. She backs away. They feign aggression. They touch and groom. He brings her gifts of food and nest-building materials. She accepts.

Suddenly, amidst cries and thunderous thrashing, the mating takes place. The earth moves. Literally.

Later that day, it's back to business as usual.

Office romances at their best can be wonderful for the people involved. Two co-workers who love each other can create a special kind of mutual support system. They can understand each other's projects and problems, offer encouragement to go for that promotion, spark each other's creativity and be there to listen after a rough day.

At their worst, though, office romances can lead to conflict, sexual harassment suits and destruction of relationships, and they can waste a lot of time. When an office romance is over, hurt feelings, anger or jealousy can make it difficult, sometimes impossible, to concentrate on the job. Too often, the participants agree that getting involved was a mistake. Yet in nearly every office, every day, people fall in love and think they have no choice in the matter.

The patterns and rules for sexuality don't come from the heart, but from the Dinosaur Brain, which comes completely programmed to run the courtship ritual on automatic pilot. Through the judicious use of hormones and neural circuitry, the brain can enforce its simple imperatives on people, making them blind to some things and unable to get other thoughts out of their minds. It can turn them into teenagers, in full view of everyone at the office. As always, the Dinosaur Brain can be fun, exciting and bad for business.

Love is difficult to deal with rationally, but when it happens at work, it's especially important to let the cortex rule, or at least consult on, the courtship. The problem is that lovesick lizards are blind. In the early stages of infatuation, nearly every couple believes that this relationship is the Real Thing and, therefore, lies outside the rules for professional behavior.

An office romance doesn't just happen and it doesn't have to end destructively. In fact, it doesn't have to end at all, if both partners understand the courtship patterns they're following and make conscious choices about their behavior. These patterns, programmed in the Dinosaur Brain, are recognizable and predictable. They are the rules by which a dinosaur gets a mate. This chapter explains how to recognize them and what to do to keep your head if you've lost your heart at the office.

Office Courtship from the Dinosaur's Point of View

Stage One: I See

Observation. The courtship pattern begins when two people start to pick each other out in a crowd. The special person appears more noticeable, somehow more three-dimensional than others. Often the cortex will try to invent reasons to explain why the other person suddenly is special.

This period can be one of high energy, confidence and self-esteem. People often find they can think more quickly and get more work done, because the Dinosaur Brain can energize people as nothing else can. It's up to them to let their cortex put the energy to good use.

Banter. After the noticing and singling out come the joking, teasing and playful aggression or competition between the two people. There's an element of conquest and aggression here that has its parallel in the dinosaur dominating its partner before the mating process begins. The competition can be good for both people, who at this stage often find themselves thinking more sharply and creatively because of the extra hormones from their Dinosaur Brains.

Display. This stage begins when people start trying to "look good." They may act differently and find themselves thinking about what they're going to wear to work on a day when they think they'll be seeing the other person. Display continues as long as the courtship does. They may realize they're spending more time on grooming, thinking about buying new clothes, or deciding to lose weight. (Dieting, by the way, is often very successful during early courtship. Appetite suppression is common.)

At this stage, co-workers might be aware that an attraction is developing. Some people can go through these early stages and be so thoroughly discreet that no one notices them, but typically, this isn't the way it happens.

Stage Two: I Want

Separating from the Herd. If the mating call has been answered with any sign of interest, the second stage of an office courtship begins. Now the couple makes active plans to be together, at first for lunches and coffee breaks, then to see each other after work. It can be a time of strong support between colleagues, of giving and getting a different viewpoint on professional problems mingled with the sweet delight of falling in love.

Fantasy. The hallmark of this stage is not just spending time together but imagining the other person when he or she isn't there.

While this fantasizing can be a source of comfort and excitement at work, it can also become a distraction that can make you seem unprofessional. The other person is with you more and more in fantasy; you address more and more behavior to this fantasized other, even though the mental images and fantasies are not necessarily sexual at this point. This stage is when the Dinosaur Brain and the cortex really start to battle it out:

Cortex: "Now wait a minute. I can't go through with this. I don't have time to get involved with anybody right now. It's not worth it."

Dinosaur Brain: "But he's so cute, and your life is so safe and boring. Here, have some more adrenaline. I want! I want!"

The key is to enjoy the Dinosaur Brain's all-for-love rush, while remembering that there's a time and place for getting the mate—but from 9 to 5 at the office, it's more important to get to work.

Arranging Meetings at Work. If the attraction is mutual, the two people begin to go out of their way to talk to or be with each other and have certain times and places where they typically meet.

People at this stage should take time to decide together how they will behave at the office. It should be understood that they won't tease or touch each other or show obvious affection or deference in public. Other people's Dinosaur Brains are alert to these signs and will know exactly what's going on. They may not realize how they know, but they know.

Confiding. As the banter falls away and the two people begin to get to know each other, they find they're getting and giving a lot of emotional support, and they like it. Their relationship doesn't have to become sexual to be satisfying.

Calling the Person at Home. A clear sign that a romance has really begun is when one person begins finding reasons to call the other at home. Usually this is for a very good business reason and it can't wait. But the telling point is this: If one of them is married and the relationship gets more serious, the calls will stop abruptly and they will never, ever call each other at home again.

Giving Gifts. Dinosaurs tend to bring tributes to their intended. Giving gifts is an instinctive phase of the courtship pattern and includes leaving notes, adding personal lines to interoffice memos and buying cute studio cards for the other person.

Touching. The Dinosaur Brain will think of ways to make physical contact and still look perfectly innocent. Hand-patting, arm-touching and neck rubs are common; hugs are rarer, unless one person has just read a Leo Buscaglia book. Denying or trying to disguise the developing relationship is part of the pattern, so it's significant if these touches look like ways of touching everyone, but aren't. (How many times do you jump at the chance to massage someone's neck?)

When touch is accompanied by lingering eye contact, the point of no return has been reached. At this step, we're getting close to the stage at which the relationship becomes overt and sexual. Until now, either person could have retreated without hurting the other's feelings. At this point, however, if someone backs off, it will be felt as a rejection.

Stage Three: I Get

Becoming Overtly Sexual. Now one of the two people wants the relationship to become sexual. They realize that they've gotten to a certain point and wonder, "Does the other really mean it? Is he (or she) as involved as I am? Just what's going on here?" They are obsessed with trying to make sense of what their Dinosaur Brains already know: A courtship pattern is going on, and both of them are following it. But what will happen next? The Dinosaur Brain knows, but the cortex is dying to find out.

Overt possessiveness may begin at this point. Often it starts as almost innocent questioning. ("Where were you yesterday?" "Do you think Sherry's pretty?") Rather than seeing it as a problem, people at this stage are often reassured by a little possessiveness in the other. They take it as a compliment. Their critical thinking is almost nonexistent.

Both people should have a clear idea of what the consequences will be if they have a sexual relationship and what the relationship will mean. It's crucial to weigh very carefully the effects of this involvement on their careers and decide how to minimize the problems it could cause at work. Getting out at this point will cause hurt feelings, but sometimes people have to cut their losses.

The Emotional Issue. Often one person will unconsciously precipitate some sort of outside event or get so worked up about something (trouble on the job can do it) that he or she will seek out the other at a time of intense emotion. Sex often follows closely.

Stage Four: I Got

The Relationship Has Become Sexual. When sex enters the picture, the Dinosaur Brain can be giddy with hormone intoxication. There are elation and infatuation, falling in love with love, the feeling that "This is just like in the movies. This is what I really want. This is the perfect relationship." Of course, at this point it really *is* the perfect relationship, because both people can leave anything at home that isn't perfect or wonderful and present only their best side to the beloved.

With their Dinosaur Brains still in control, the lovers feel like teenagers, and in many ways they act like teenagers, stealing time together, cutting out on work, hiding behind closed office doors, touching feet under tables and giving each other surreptitious hugs in corridors. They will often assume at this point that no one knows about their connection because they are being so discreet. Actually, they are anything but discreet.

The Dinosaur Brain is proud of its conquest and wants to strut. This is a serious mistake for people at work. Nobody else needs to know the intimate details of a romance. Kissing and telling can leave people's professional reputations in ruins.

Once the relationship has become sexual, the couple needs to decide what they're going to do about it. In some cases, they might decide that they don't really want an affair and take steps to end it right away. But if they've taken time to think it through, being involved can be positive. The couple can be strong supports for each other, sharing their professional territory as well as their personal lives. They can learn to work together, with each staking out certain dominant areas within the professional relationship. It's possible to be colleagues and lovers, but each person needs a separate area of power.

Territory. When an office romance is in full bloom, the higher-status person in the relationship might rearrange things so that his or her lover can be closer. This could involve a transfer or reassignment to the same department and often indicates a profound lack of foresight.

The temptation is strong to bring a lover into your territory at work. Don't do it! Even the appearance of favoritism can be a real problem. Worse can be the problems that ensue if the affair ends and the other person is still right there.

It can also be easy to get involved in an affair with someone you supervise. Attraction can be confused with submission to a dominant figure. This is the recipe for exploitation. It's not a good idea to become romantically involved with someone you supervise; the effects on both careers can be very damaging. Your Dinosaur Brain may send you attraction signals; you must use your cortex to avoid acting on them.

On and Off. The most difficult phase of a courtship may be the on-again, off-again stage, where one or both people are ambivalent about what will happen and what they want. One day it's go further; the next day, retreat. This time is the most destructive in an office romance, and this problem gives office romance its bad name. People in this stage have an especially hard time remembering that it's imperative to make work off-limits for discussing the relationship. The Dinosaur Brain is always saying, "I don't care if you are in a meeting, we have to get this settled right now!"

Stage Five: I Go/I Stay

Eventually in any office romance, reality intrudes. It may be anything from the first slight, perhaps a forgotten birthday or a canceled lunch date, to something major such as marital problems or one of the lovers having doubts. This is the time that makes or breaks the relationship because often people didn't bargain for getting involved with a living, breathing other person.

The magic fades. The premating excitement, which the Dinosaur Brain supplied before sex, eventually decreases when mating has occurred. It's easiest if it happens for both people at the same time, but, sadly, that is seldom the case. If the relationship is to continue, it will require something besides magic.

At this point people must ask seriously, "Is this the Real Thing?" It's not easy to tell yet if the love affair will last and turn into something more permanent, because love takes time to develop and grow, but it's possible to tell if it's not. If both people don't begin making difficult choices here and now, it's not the Real Thing.

This stage is when a couple's personal lives can seriously affect their careers. There are decisions to be made, and the Dinosaur Brain does not deal well with pressure and stress. If the relationship is to work, the cortex must take charge. Only the cortex can supply empathy, respect and compromise, which are the foundation of lasting love. Without them, the Reptile Response will express itself with possessiveness, jealousy and utter distraction.

Married Lovers

If one person is married and has loyalties to two different people, there can be particular stress and few easy answers. The longer the situation is allowed to go unresolved, the more distracting it can be to doing one's job. People in this situation need to evaluate their options clearly, make as rational a decision as possible, and stick to their choice. The Dinosaur Brain will always want what's attractive and available, even if its quest is rewarded only part time.

If there is a spouse involved who hasn't found out yet, it's pretty sure that he or she will. The Dinosaur Brain is not capable of re-

solving this kind of situation. It wants both. To avoid endless vac-
illation, the cortex has to make the decision, take the action and
stick with it. No, there's no other way.

Chapter 25 explores some of the ways to tell if this affair is the Real
Thing or just another office romance. But here it's important to
consider what you'll do if you need to break it off.

Termination

When a relationship ends and both people realize that it's over,
there can be a painful period of mourning that includes sadness,
apathy, anger, sometimes difficulty in sleeping, eating disturbances
and inability to concentrate at work.

When the romance is over, at least one of the people may have to
pick up the pieces, professionally as well as romantically. Careers
have been damaged by the Dinosaur Brain's singlemindedness in
getting the mate. Here's what to do to switch from Dinosaur Brain
to cortical thinking after the end of an unfortunate office romance.

Plan One: Image Assessment

1. It's helpful to have a close friend with you for this step, because
it's very difficult to do it yourself. First, find out how much people
know. Most developing office romances are predictable to other
people before they're predictable to the couple involved. Give your
friend permission to tell you all the gory details, snide comments,
rumors, and so forth. You need to know. See how much people
have figured out and what they're saying about you.

2. Whatever you hear, assume it's 30 percent worse than what
you've been told, because even your best friend won't reveal the
worst of the rumors or the most dire of his or her suspicions.

3. To find out how badly the romance has affected your career,
try to make a few minor requests and see if they're acted on in just
the same way as they always were.

4. If you have an understanding boss or a mentor, it's good to ask for advice, but if you ask for advice in this situation, you need to take it. If a transfer is possible, or a reassignment to another work area can be made without too much of a problem, that's the best choice.

5. If someone above you in the company hierarchy tells you that your career is damaged, or if you get a peculiar answer to a request and something perfectly reasonable is not granted, it's probably time to move on.

6. If you stay where you are, you might want to go to Plan Two, which is to act straighter than the straightest people at work. You have to realize that you have a public relations problem, and in P.R., the truth is less important than the appearance of truth.

Plan Two: Straight Arrow

1. No flirting. Not only must you not flirt, you must not even appear to do so. Don't even stop to say "Hello" to an attractive member of the opposite sex. When he or she walks by, turn your head the other way.

2. Keep your emotions toned down. Deal with your mourning away from the office. See a therapist if you need to.

3. Focus on business, and let everyone know you're focusing on business. It wouldn't hurt to drop a few comments here and there about how you stayed late to work on a certain contract last night or how you're already three points ahead of your quota.

4. Drop hints about your stable home and family life. Tell people that you and your spouse are going to take a long vacation or are planning an addition to the house. If you're not married, don't talk about relationships at all.

5. Don't explain your side of the affair to anyone, no matter what, especially if there are bad feelings between you and your former lover. Just say it was a mistake and leave it at that.

6. Don't do it again.

8

If It Hurts, Hiss!

A group of herbivores is peacefully mucking the greens at the edge of the swamp for such food as they can find. The day is hot; the pace is languid. They do what they do with the dreamy intensity possible only when you have absolutely nothing on your mind.

Something changes. A strange sound, a strange smell. Something doesn't feel right. Danger. The warning cry fairly bursts from their throats as they scatter to hide.

Our cries of danger and pain are complaints and accusations. They began as protective signals but now, with the advent of language, they've turned into devices that structure reality, rather than responses to reality.

The Dinosaur Brain says, "When something is wrong, let people know—seek out the villain, drive out the intruder, punish the sinner. There is no virtue in suffering in silence." This response really has two parts: the blaming and the telling about it.

When mistakes are made in business, the impulse is to find out who is to blame and to punish that person. This behavior gets in the way of progress, because the way we learn usually is by trial and error. Yet in many situations we act as if what we expect is trial and success, or trial and punishment. Blame is a destructive concept on both corporate and individual levels.

Corporate-Level Blame

Let's start with the corporate level. We refuse to learn anything from losers.

Bob, a division head in a computer firm, makes some decisions about a new software line and comes out with the right product at the right time. He makes a bundle, The Wall Street Journal *writes about his brilliant success and Bob becomes a hero.*

In another five years, he goes through the same process with another software package, but this time his product is a real dud and just doesn't sell. What happens next? Somebody takes a fall—either Bob himself or, if he's a shrewd enough old dinosaur, maybe he can shift the blame to the marketing department or the people in production.

When a decision goes awry, we tend to focus on the people who made it, rather than on the decision itself. Our assumption, which is really unwarranted, is that good people make good decisions, and vice versa. The Dinosaur Brain doesn't care about learning because it can't learn. People who use their cortexes can learn to make good decisions if they analyze the old ones and recognize which were the successful parts and which the unsuccessful.

Decisions are complex cognitive tasks rather than signs of grace. Maybe executives in responsible positions should be required to keep logs, as sea captains do. After each decision, a manager would list his or her reasons for having made it and record how it turned out. A living document such as this would be a great aid to the manager and company.

Usually the only information we have about how and why decisions were made is in the self-serving memoirs of great managers, which leave us feeling that some people just have it and others don't. But what is "it?" We have very little vocabulary for talking about internal thought processes. Decisions feel as if they jump fully grown from one's head. It takes some work to backtrack the path that the mind skipped down so easily. This is a job for a corporate historian.

For example, what if we assumed that Bob was a reasonable person, and we took a look at the elements that entered into his decision, the information he had and what he did with that information? What if we learned from his mistakes instead of punishing someone for making them?

Decisions can be tracked, and we can learn from them, but we need to abandon the idea that making mistakes is evidence of a character flaw. We need to involve our cortex, not only in making decisions, but in evaluating them after they're made.

The concept of blame has a number of negative effects in the corporate world. First, it keeps people from taking risks. Cover Your Tail becomes the name of the game in the land of the dinosaurs. If something new comes out, people immediately start looking for back doors, ways to dissociate themselves from the project in case it fails. This attitude tends to split the corporate team. People will withhold information and keep something in reserve to protect themselves in case things go wrong, which, of course, makes it more likely that something will go wrong.

Placing blame also tends to breed an air of paranoia and plays into more destructive Dinosaur Brain tactics, such as trying to eliminate rivals for top positions. It also contributes to the internal competition that can make companies more vulnerable to competition from the outside. A company suffers if it does not function as a single unit. Certainly enough sports metaphors are used in corporate board rooms that we are aware of the value of team play.

Personalized Blame

The concept of blame does the most damage on the personal side. To see how this works, we have to advance into the realm of epistemology, the study of how we know what we know. I'll start by asking an easy question: What is reality?

You don't need to think too long about your answer. Reality is simply what we think it is. There are lots of facts and objective information out there, but in the end, what defines psychological realness is nothing more than our belief in it. I'm not talking about the laws of physics but of how our minds work. We see what we expect to see. If we look for something new, we find it and can learn from it. Of course, the Dinosaur Brain never looks for anything new because it knows all it needs to know already.

Richard was not picked for promotion. He knows that Carl was moved up because Carl plays golf with the boss and is always volunteering to serve on those silly committees. Carl's just a brownnoser, that's all. Richard has five years on him, but it just goes to show that it isn't what you know, it's who you know.

Richard repeats that story again and again to whomever will listen. Each time he tells it with more feeling and conviction. Each repetition makes it more real to him. What started out as an opinion ends up as truth.

Let's look at the reality that Richard is creating for himself. First, his Dinosaur Brain instinct to blame rather than learn tells him he's the victim of a corrupt system. His ego is protected at the expense of his career. He has less motivation to continue doing a good job. In his eyes, the good job he did was punished, not rewarded, which proves the system is corrupt.

Richard is missing an obvious fact: If you want to get promoted, you have to promote yourself. What he calls Carl's brownnosing may be just an indication that Carl has a better understanding of how the system works.

The first component of the "If it hurts, hiss" response is to find someone to blame. The second is the compulsion to talk about it. Our Dinosaur Brain is programmed to warn people of danger and to repeat the cry over and over. If there's nobody there to tell, we repeat it to ourselves, over and over, and each time it seems more true.

Let's look at what this way of thinking does inside Richard. Every time he thinks about or repeats the promotion story, his brain, which doesn't know reality from fantasy, reacts as if this affront were happening right then. Richard goes into the Triple F response: His body wears itself out; his stomach continues to churn and secrete acid; he is quite literally poisoning himself with his own resentment. Take it from a psychotherapist; this is the way that people drive themselves crazy.

Richard's "Hiss" response is cheating him out of the element that is most important to mental health and resistance to disease and stress: the feeling that he is in control of his own life. He thinks there is nothing he can do, that he is a victim. Is Richard the victim of a corrupt system or of his own patterns of thinking?

The dinosaur never sees itself as the source of any of its troubles. Whenever something goes wrong, the dinosaur's response is to find somebody else to blame and then complain about it. The dinosaur is always eager to compare notes with fellow sufferers and to defend itself from any criticism.

The monthly printout showed that Jason's department was hip-deep in red ink. Within an hour, Jason had prepared a rebuttal memo and carried it personally to his supervisor. Everything was neatly listed and documented with examples: who had missed a deadline and had to work overtime; whose expense accounts were suspect; who had an attitude problem; who was dawdling on purpose to make Jason look bad; who had authorized purchases when Jason was out of town. There was no way the boss could pin the deficit on him.

Jason's Dinosaur Brain told him to find the culprits. He ignored the fact that he was supposed to be in charge. This is also a classic example of "flight" tactics. Jason twisted reality so that he saw himself as a victim of his subordinates. His Dinosaur Brain is leading the way toward paranoia. It has no regard for what others might think is happening, only what fits its own patterns.

Yet, we can instinctively understand Jason's reaction. We all have the impulse to blame others when the chips are down. Our Dinosaur Brain tells us that mistakes are capital offenses. Sometimes the Dinosaur Brain is right. What would it be like to work in a company like Jason's? How willing would you be to do your best job or to commit yourself to anything if you knew that, as soon as a mistake was made, unless your tail was the one that was most thoroughly covered, it would end up in a sling?

Gossip and Complaints— the Telling Component

People love gossip, and gossip is almost never about the good things that others do.

Sheryl delights in being the bearer of bad news. Her theme song is, "Listen to what the guys in the front office have done this time." She then recounts the latest human rights violation committed by the people in finance.

Her Dinosaur Brain believes that her cry of pain obligates you to help and protect her by joining her war against the number crunchers.

You may feel some hostility against those nefarious penny-pinchers yourself, but consider the disadvantages of going to war with them. They are, after all, part of the same company, and you're all on the same team. But if you continue to listen to Sheryl and, worse, join in her game of "Can You Top This?" you're apt to find yourself in a conflict with finance that is really not to your advantage. Not only that, it's a conflict that's being run very poorly. Griping alone never overthrew a tyrant.

If you share stories with Sheryl, you can be pretty sure they will get back to the finance department. Most likely, they will think of more effective ways to retaliate than Sheryl does. If you listen to her and share your own resentment with her, she will assume you agree and that you're on her side against them.

Once you start playing the complaining game, you find that your feelings toward the finance department, your boss or whomever is the target begin to change. What started out as an innocent gripe session can really cause problems to your morale.

When you work with someone like Sheryl, be very careful not to give any indication that you agree with what she says. Remember, too, that hissing and telling can also kill your chances for a promotion.

Dinosaurs are very vocal about their pain. Dissatisfied dinosaurs tend to form support groups in which they're actually supporting each other's distorted view of reality. The group is merely an environment in which they can complain. The Dinosaur Brain believes that complaining is doing something about a bad situation. If that were true, the gripers would have inherited the Earth long ago.

Talking about problems can get us support and help from other people, which is sometimes just what we need. We wouldn't be social creatures if we didn't complain. However, "getting it off your chest" disguised as taking action can bleed off the energy you need to actually do something about a situation.

Of course, it can be helpful to talk out certain feelings, especially losses and sadness. With other emotions, especially hurt and anger, it's best to express your feelings once to someone you care about and trust. When you do it repeatedly and to everybody, you're not talking to others; you're talking to yourself and creating justification for your Dinosaur Brain's resentment and perception of victimization.

What to Do

Now let's look at these companion notions of blaming and complaining, and find out what to do about them in yourself and others. First, in yourself:

1. Ask yourself, when you start thinking in terms of blame, "When I know who's to blame, what will I have? What will I gain by punishing someone for this? Why is thinking this way to my advantage?"

If you aren't satisfied with your answers, ask, "How else could I look at the situation? What can I learn here? Will I really make it better by finding someone to blame?"

2. Check your goals. When you hear yourself complaining or blaming, ask, "Why am I saying this? What is my goal here? What

effect will this comment have on the people listening to me? What kind of reaction do I expect? Do I want them to agree with me? Rescue me? Divert their attention from me and attack somebody else? What am I trying to accomplish? Am I really doing something or just pretending?" Decide what action you could take to make the situation better, then put up or shut up.

3. Recognize your own repetitious mental programs and know how to change the channel on your internal television. Repeating the same stories to yourself will only make you more upset and angry.

You might want to try this thought-stopping technique: Put a rubber band around your wrist and, every time you find yourself repeating one of these blaming-and-complaining tapes, snap the rubber band. This device focuses your attention on deciding what you really want to do.

4. Look inside and ask yourself how you forgive people. For most of us, forgiveness involves concentrating on the value of the person and our feelings of attachment to him or her. Blame ultimately ends in driving off or destroying someone. If you think about the person's value, you might have less desire to destroy.

Some people tend to blame themselves when anything goes wrong at work. What they're doing basically is dividing themselves into two people: one who is "me" and the other who is "not me." Then they try to drive off or punish the part that is "not me" and come up with a feeling of guilt.

Whenever there's guilt, there is also resentment of whatever makes us feel guilty, an outsider or a part of ourselves. This internal division of the personality into good and bad parts is the essence of neurosis. Forgiving yourself is as crucial for mental health as forgiving others.

Here's how to deal with other people who blame and complain:

1. Practice "creative ignoring." When you're surrounded by a crowd of people who are screaming, yelling and demanding somebody's head, just sit there. This response is much more thought-out and creative than agreeing with them.

2. Answer bad with good. Whatever someone complains about, bring up a good point. This might get the complainer to stop and think. (Of course, it might also make him attack you.) If he or she does stop and think, the person will be moving a bit out of the Dinosaur Brain and into the cortex.

Answering bad with good is also a good way to cover your tail. People who remember the situation later might see you as the only one who didn't lose his or her head. You might be considered the leader when everybody calms down.

3. When people come to you, expecting you to agree with them or rescue them, ask them the magic question, "What are you going to do about it?" If they expected you to take on their problem, this will stop them dead in their tracks. They will have to think about just exactly what is going on and what they expect, thereby engaging their cortex. You may not have much control over how they structure the world, but you don't have to accept their structure as your own.

9

Like Me, Good; Not Like Me, Bad

Let's face it. There are two kinds of people in the world. Some people believe in working hard for what they get; they're industrious and dependable. They take pride in their ability to do a solid day's work. They get behind the things they believe in and make those things a part of their lives. They're responsible, warm and caring. They provide for their families and for those less fortunate in their community.

Then there are the other people out there who want everything handed to them. They don't particularly care about doing a good job, only that they get what's coming to them. They put themselves first in everything, and everybody else can just go to hell. They don't value being dependable and trustworthy. All they want is to have fun and get what they can.

Maybe you know what to call the kinds of people I'm talking about. If you do, you know firsthand how your Dinosaur Brain can distort reality. There is nothing in the world easier to believe and less true than the classification I just proposed.

Read it again. There is really no concrete information, there are no facts, and the adjectives are vague, but all the statements have strong moral connotations. Which group did you put yourself in? If you're like most people, you easily saw yourself in the first category and other people in the second.

It feels as if I said something real, but there's actually nothing there except a two-category classification that breaks down into good and evil. Like me, good; not like me, bad. That's the essence of Dinosaur Brain thinking, and it pervades the human consciousness.

All the great crimes of humanity are based on this tendency to classify into two categories. This classification is the neurological basis for prejudice, racism, genocide and wars. Go back to the opening paragraph. Whom did you think I was talking about? The very arguments I presented have been advanced as justification for killing Jews, enslaving blacks, not allowing Hispanics or other foreigners to enter this country, or going to war with virtually anybody.

Most of us have enough cortical control to avoid a two-category view of the world, but when we let our Dinosaur Brains take over, the system breaks down into good guys (us) versus bad guys (anyone not like us).

Many problems on the job arise because people operate on faith. They "just know" that there are two ways to do things, a right way and a wrong way. As discussed in Chapter 32, blind faith is no way to run a business. People need to get along with each other at the office, but if their Dinosaur Brains control their lives, the result can be factionalism, feuds and personality clashes.

What do you do about this kind of good-versus-bad classification system? First, be on the lookout for it, especially during a conflict. Check inside to see if you're really mad at what the person is rather than what he or she has done.

Realize that your Dinosaur Brain tends to see the world in terms of black and white or right and wrong and that this view may have nothing to do with the facts of the case. Demand facts as the basis for your decision.

There's no way to avoid classification completely. (My telling you that there's a right and a wrong way to make decisions shows that I do it too.) We must, however, be aware of its ability to limit how we see the world. If you find yourself consciously using a two-category system, be aware that you're really talking right versus wrong.

Classification systems come up most often in our lives as an unspoken basis for our thinking. This problem has many faces, some of which you might see day-to-day on your job.

The Personality Clash. Donna and Sharon, her boss, hate each other. Donna sees Sharon as a tyrant who makes arbitrary decisions and who rose in the hierarchy for some unknown reason, certainly not ability. Donna thinks Sharon's real problem is that she's just basically stupid, and Donna's not about to be pushed around by somebody who's not nearly as smart as she is.

Sharon sees Donna as arrogant and ill-tempered. She overreacts to everything and, whatever she wants Donna to do, Donna wants to do the opposite. There's no way she can give her any direction without offending her. Donna always thinks she knows better. Sharon would really like to get rid of her, but federal regulations and lawsuits being what they are, there's no capital offense she can pin on her.

Sharon just hopes that keeping the pressure up, day in and day out, will make Donna want to quit. Donna, for her part, is never going to let a two-bit idiot drive her out of her job.

Donna's classification involves people who are stupid versus people who are intelligent. For her, bosses often fit in the former category and employees in the latter. Sharon's categories probably involve people who don't accept direction versus people who do. It's easy to see into which she thinks Donna fits.

This situation can persist for years. It can divide an office into factions and cause ulcers and lawsuits. What has to happen here will be very difficult for Donna and Sharon. They must start seeing each other as people who are working together on the same projects, doing the same job. They have to see their similarities and common purposes and learn to be happy with each other, rather than right.

It is nearly impossible to get people to change thinking by themselves. If you manage people like this, you need to show them that they're not getting anywhere dealing with each other as they have been, and if they want to keep their sanity, they need to find another way. The solution involves focusing on behavior rather than personality or attitudes. This issue is discussed more fully in Chapter 33.

You could teach Donna, for example, to play the role of politician. Tell her to be a conscious phony so she can get the same rewards as the other phonies. This would take the heat off her and reduce the number of reprimands she'd have to deal with.

Sharon would need to realize that hating Donna is a luxury she can't afford. She may want to get rid of this particular problem, but there will be other Donnas. It might be helpful to have her compare Donna mentally to a piece of equipment that's constantly in need of adjustment but isn't bad enough to be scrapped. Adjusting is a supervisor's job. If the equipment always runs right, all you need is someone to turn it on.

If you have to handle a feud like this, you can't ignore their senses of right and wrong. If you tell either of them, "Oh, Sharon isn't such a bad apple" or "Donna is really a nice person," they'll just look at you as if you're crazy. What you have to say is, "I don't care how bad she is, you can make the situation better for yourself."

Your own Dinosaur Brain will beg you to take sides. Don't listen. You could turn the feud into a class struggle.

The Workaholic Ethic. Adam is a classic workaholic. He keeps incredible hours: in at 7 A.M. and out sometimes at 8 or 9 at night. He gets a lot accomplished but at great cost. If he takes a break or goes on vacation, he considers himself lazy and usually just spends the time thinking about the things he has to do at the office. Even his hobbies involve a lot of work.

Adam divides his life into what is important and what is unimportant. The important stuff is work, money, achievement, duty; the unimportant is everything else. His family devoutly wishes that their concerns and feelings would get onto his important list.

We used to write off people like Adam by saying, "Oh, he'll just work himself to death and have a heart attack." That was the value system of the 1960s and 1970s coming up in our own Dinosaur

Brains, classifying people into good and bad and imagining a heart attack as a punishment for evil, rather than a disease.

More recent research and more recent values suggest that perhaps Adam is no more likely to die of a heart attack than people who goof off more, especially if he doesn't have any particular temper problems. Nevertheless, the careers of people such as Adam have several flaws.

First, Adam is unable to see the big picture. Usually people like Adam get hung up on details, and sometimes they miss out on seeing larger patterns, such as the things that would make their jobs easier. The truth is that making their jobs easier is of no value to them. They value things that involve hard work and long hours.

Second, these workaholics tend to fall prey to perfectionism. They must do every job, no matter how small, exactly right. Since there are only 24 hours in the day, people have to decide which tasks they'll perform in kind of a half-baked way, or else they'd never get anything done. Not Adam. The Adams of the world are definitely not efficient; they spend a lot of time perfecting things that may not warrant the perfection.

Finally, the biggest flaw in workaholics is their difficulty in dealing with other people. If others aren't as willing to work as hard as they do, the workaholics see it as evidence of the mortal sin, laziness. Their attitude is: What can you do with lazy people except fire them or delegate to them the most menial of tasks, and supervise them constantly to see that they don't goof off?

Perfectionists also often have tremendous irritability problems, which does nothing to improve their skills as managers. For them, management has nothing to do with how people feel; they belong to the "just *do* it" school of management theory. Good people do it; lazy people don't. They are always surprised, shocked and angry about just how irresponsible people can be. They can't see that their own irritability is a major reason that people don't want to do what they say.

If you supervise someone like Adam, you need to enter his classification system and tell him that managing difficult people is something that's valuable but very hard to do. You might intimate that

Adam might not be willing to make the effort to learn to get along with others. What workaholic can resist that challenge? (Actually, plenty can. They say, "I'm paid to be a manager here and I would be able to manage if people would stop knocking on my door and asking me about their problems.")

If you have a boss like Adam, you need to realize that our corporate society currently regards workaholism as positive, and there isn't really very much you can do to change him. You won't be able to convince him that there is anything wrong with what he's doing, so don't even try. If you were Adam's wife or child, you probably wouldn't be able to convince him either.

The best thing to do is to negotiate with him for tasks to accomplish, rather than for how much time you're required to spend on an assignment. You might well be more efficient than he is, so maybe you can accomplish everything he wants you to do, rather than having him require you to be at work half the night or on Saturdays. Always look busy!

Workaholics are notorious for demanding that other people do exactly as they do. The more you can keep Adam focused on the final product rather than on time spent or attitude, the better things will go. Be careful, though, because typically people like this will raise the ante. If you can do your assigned work in half a day, Adam might double your workload rather than reward you for efficiency. The more the requirements are spelled out, the safer you'll be.

If you are like Adam, you might have begun to see some problems in being that way. We have already mentioned possible problems with efficiency and interpersonal relationships, but there is also a psychological toll to consider. Workaholics usually are profoundly lonely.

Do you agree that "If you want something done right, you have to do it yourself"? Think about the contempt for other people and the loneliness implied in that statement. The big problem for people like Adam is in simply being able to enjoy life. They consider all of life's little joys either bad or unimportant. Don't worry. I won't turn this into a sermon. If you haven't been convinced in your own life, I won't be able to convince you in the pages of a book. Besides, I don't think you're willing to put out the extra effort it takes to change your behavior.

If you are like Adam and you want to change, you can do several things. The best plan is to use a schedule. Set aside certain times for work and certain times for play. Don't work any longer than the time scheduled. At first you'll feel very anxious, but later you'll begin to learn pacing and efficiency.

Schedule time to play and be with your family. You'll feel lost for awhile and will find yourself thinking about all the work you could be doing, but stick with it.

Realize that the workaholic syndrome is your problem, not your chief asset, especially in being a manager. A manager's main job is to motivate people. If you find yourself thinking of your employees as lazy, no-account, shiftless, and so forth, realize this is your Dinosaur Brain talking. You won't get anybody to do anything by lecturing, as you well know if you're already discounting the lecture you just read.

The Burnout Syndrome. Burnout is the only disorder I know that was named by the people who have it. They would like you to believe that it's a disorder caused by the job and that they have just given and given until there was nothing left, and they burned out in a blaze of glory. That, of course, is an enticing trap for people who believe that giving is better than taking.

Burnout is actually a moral disorder, based on the two-category system of givers versus takers. People with burnout aren't really workaholics who are overworking themselves; they are people who have made a bargain with life, and the bargain is not being kept.

Louisa is always doing things for other people. She's considered the department mother, baking cookies for the staff, spending time talking with people who need her, helping, working her fingers to the bone. Yet these are the things she considers important.

Louisa thinks her boss and her company are cold-hearted, more concerned about the bottom line than about the people who work for them. She feels it's her personal job to go around behind her boss every time he tells people to do something, finding out how they're feeling about it. Louisa implies by her actions that the boss doesn't know what he's doing and he just doesn't care.

Her personal tragedy is that people just don't care as much about her as she does about them. She is a giver, and the rest of the world is made up of takers. Everybody—her fellow employees, her friends, her children—comes to Louisa to tell their problems, but when she has a problem, is anybody there? No. She suffers in silence. You wouldn't believe how many physical ailments she has, and each day she grows steadily more and more depressed.

Louisa believes that if people are good, they will return consideration in kind. She has never discussed this with anybody, but she's just more and more sure that there are only a few nice people in the world, and she is one of the last of them.

Louisa is typical of the kind of people who diagnose themselves as victims of burnout or come up with its symptoms. These people, especially those who work in the social services, believe that what they define as good behavior will be rewarded, regardless of the company's (or the world's) priorities. They define what's good and reasonable for them to do, then feel that their bosses jump all over them and tell them to spend their time doing something more productive. Louisa cannot see the aggression and anger in her own behavior. She never gets angry. She gets other people angry at her.

People like Louisa also practice the kind of manipulation that involves giving to others and expecting them to give back. She spends a lot of time feeling let down and blames it on her job, which is much easier than adjusting her own behavior to focus on the kind of work she considers unimportant and that her boss considers productive. The Dinosaur Brain strikes again.

The Wrong Job. Now let's look at a person who is undermining her career by not committing herself to what she considers the Wrong Job.

Sarah is sure that as soon as she finds the right job, she will rise straight to the top. She has a degree from a prestigious business school and is an expert on management information systems. So far she's been hired by four different companies.

Each started by talking about her in glowing terms and promising they would be getting on board with a state-of-the-art management information system. As time went on, however, Sarah found more and more resistance from the staff and little support from management.

She feels that the people she reported to were much more interested in playing politics than in getting the kind of system she could develop for them. She always ends up wishing they would just let her do what she was trained to do, but nobody will. She sees the resistance she has met as arising out of ignorance. Management information systems are the coming thing and every company needs one. She is exasperated at how backward the thinking is in the companies she has worked for. She just hopes that, if she gets to a big enough and modern enough company, her talents will be recognized and appreciated.

Sarah doesn't realize that any job has formal and informal aspects. The formal aspects are what you are paid to do, such as designing and running a management information system. The informal aspects are what you have to do to be allowed to do your job, which, at most companies, means politics.

Sarah doesn't see that she must sell her ideas and work to make other people believe what she already knows is right. Instead, she just assumes that she's meeting a lot of people who have moral or intellectual flaws. This is typical Dinosaur Brain thinking.

The situation has spiraled at each of her jobs, until Sarah has started looking for work at a fifth company. She is bright and sells herself well (in the interviews, because that's OK), but before too long her lack of a track record will catch up with her. She keeps repeating the same pattern, thinking that she is just in the Wrong Job and feeling disillusioned about how hard it is to get people to let her implement a new idea. She just can't bring herself to try to sell something to people who are so stupid that they can't see its value without being told.

Sarah lacks commitment. Solidity, character and success can come from treating the job you have as if it were the right one. (Of course,

I've also seen people who stick through thick and thin with obviously bad jobs, so you need to look carefully at your own situation.)

If you see that you're always in the wrong job, learn to make a decision and stick with it, whether you feel that it's right or wrong later. If you work at a job as if it were a good one, you'll be much more likely to get a better one.

PART III

Using Lizard Logic

10

Avoiding the Reptile Response

Have you ever found yourself face to face with an enraged boss, client or colleague? It's not a pleasant situation, and it can play havoc with your career. The only real way to win an argument at work is to stop it as quickly as possible by muzzling your Dinosaur Brain and settling the dispute rationally.

That's easy to say but difficult to do. And the reason it's hard has more to do with your brain than the situation. Your brain is programmed to respond to aggression in one of three ways: by fighting back, running away or becoming immobilized. As we learned in Chapter 4, this programming, the Triple F Response, is an evolutionary relic that goes back to the age of the dinosaurs.

Business is not the jungle. The victor is not the person who yells the loudest but the one who stays the coolest. The way to win an argument at work is to avoid the Reptile Response pattern. Here's how:

Ask for Time to Stop and Think. No one will get angrier if you say, "Wait a minute. I need to think before I answer." This pause often will have a calming effect on the other person as well.

Listen to Your Heart, Literally. If your heart rate is up, be careful. The more aroused you are, the less clearly you can think, and the more likely you are to fall into a Reptile Response pattern yourself.

In general, if your heart rate is more than 100 beats per minute, beware. There are several ways to monitor this. If you're into running or aerobics, you already know the methods. For others, an easy guideline is, if you're aware of your heart beating fast, calm down. Other signs of arousal were discussed in Chapter 4.

Take the time and effort to calm yourself. Take a deep breath, sit down, count to ten or whatever it takes to lower your arousal.

Hold Your Immediate Response. Even if a perfect rejoinder is fairly leaping out of your mouth, don't say it! Your first response will almost always be a Dinosaur Brain fight-or-flight reaction:

"Says you!"

"I did not!"

"You didn't tell me that before!"

"These figures are wrong!"

"What I said was. . . ."

All of these are Reptile Responses in the attack-defense mode and will make the other person angrier.

Also when someone is angry at you, you need to consider your strategy. There's no point in giving away your position or letting the other person know you're upset until you've completely thought it through. Let somebody else jump to conclusions. The dinosaur with the most rope often ends up dangling from the end of it.

Ask Yourself, "What Do I Want to Happen?" Base your actions on your goal. Think the situation through before committing yourself to a response.

If the Other Person Is Yelling, Don't Do Anything Until You Get Him or Her to Stop. Keep your own voice soft, and ask the person to calm down, if that is appropriate.

I ask people, "Please don't yell," but sometimes that wording can backfire on you. Instead you can ask, "Could you run that by a bit more slowly this time?" (Have you ever tried to yell slowly?) This approach will get the person to focus on the content, instead of the decibel level.

A calm, quiet manner is usually your best bet. A rabbi once said, "A soft answer turneth away wrath."

On the telephone, you can interrupt without saying a word if you remember the "uh huh" rule. We usually respond with "uh huh" when the other person takes a breath. If you can wait through three breaths without saying "uh huh," the other person will usually stop and ask if you are still there. This is a good time to say, "Could you run that by a bit more slowly?"

Remember That Explaining Your Point of View Will Not Help. All too often, explanations are disguised forms of fighting back or running away:

Fighting back. "I've been doing this job for twenty years, and nobody's had that problem before." This response obviously means, "You are the stupidest person I've seen in twenty years." It's an attack and will be understood as such.

What possible good would it do for the other person to know that no one else has had this problem? He or she has the problem and that's all that's important.

Any statement that does not give useful information is your Dinosaur Brain talking. Questions whose goals are to give rather than receive information are also Dinosaur Brain statements, such as "Do you realize that the boss may not like this?"

Running away. It's a well-known fact that 99.82 percent of all mistakes in American business come from one of two sources: the computer or "the new girl" or guy.

When you tell people that, do they yell at whoever made the mistake? No. They just yell louder at you. They feel they are getting the runaround. They aren't interested in whose fault it is, you are. They want to know how you're going to fix the mistake.

Explanations mostly are a way of saying, "I'm right. I'm a good person." You need to make an effort to save the other person's face. Being right is a way of winning. Structuring the situation so that you win turns the other person into the loser.

Don't explain unless knowing the explanation would help solve the problem. If you must explain, at least do it after you've asked what the other person wants.

Let the Other Person Know You Hear. Restate what you heard. Let the other person know you can understand why he or she might be upset. Here are some ways to do it:

"So, as I understand it, you're upset because I rated you 'satisfactory' rather than excellent."

"The thing that's hanging us up, then, is what's going to happen if that order doesn't get there by the deadline."

"You feel I didn't back you up in the planning meeting."

"I can see how you'd be upset."

"That would tick me off too."

Restating does two things. It clarifies the problem so you both understand and agree on its nature. It also lets the other person know that you think what he or she is saying is worth listening to. It's a compliment and it saves face.

Ask, "What Would You Like Me to Do?" Be careful about placing the emphasis on the word "like" or "do," not on "me." Listen to the answer, and state it back to make sure you got it right.

People have to stop and think to answer this question. They have to move from the Dinosaur Brain to the cortex.

State What You Want. Avoid telling people what they are doing, what they have done, or the ways in which they are acting like lizards. This will only get you an argument about whether they really are acting this way. Instead, use one of these approaches:

"I would like us to come to a workable agreement." (Not "You're being unreasonable.")

"I'd like to pay you $2.20 apiece for the lot of ten thousand." (Not "You charge too much.")

"I'd like us both to go away feeling like winners." (Not "You're a hard-headed SOB.")

"I'd like to leave this meeting with a feeling that I'm valuable to this organization." (Not "You don't appreciate me.")

The Dinosaur Brain will hear any sentence that begins with "you are" (real or implied) as an attack and will defend against it.

Negotiate. Many books are available on how to negotiate well. For our purposes, the steps to effective negotiation are as follows:

"As I understand it, you want. . . ."

"I want. . . ."

"I'm willing to offer X if you're willing to give Y."

Counter until you reach an agreement.

Get Verbal Acknowledgement of What You Both Have Agreed to Do. Some examples:

"So we're agreed that if I complete the project by March 15, I get a ten percent raise."

"It's understood, then, that we'll pay $2.50 for the first ten thousand if you cut the price by 25¢ on the next twenty thousand that we purchase during this calendar year."

"I will try to give you more verbal support, and you'll try to be more punctual. Let's meet again in two weeks and see how we're doing."

The last example illustrates another important aspect of this technique. Set some sort of time frame to review your decision. Not only is this good business sense, but it also gives each of you another chance to discuss your agreement and make any needed modifications rationally and without raised voices.

Let the Other Person Have the Last Word, If at All Possible. Sometimes the Dinosaur Brain can't resist a parting shot that could undo all the good that's been done. Remember, having the last word is an aggressive act.

11

Bad Moods and Internal Television

It's no secret that negative thoughts lead to bad moods. So, if you don't want to get into bad moods, don't think bad thoughts.

For many people, it's not that easy. They don't realize that they have any control over what they think. For them the thoughts just come from somewhere else, and they have to watch whatever's on—like TV.

Thoughts really are like TV, but you produce all the programs and decide what to watch. If you're not as happy as you'd like to be, maybe it has something to do with the quality of your programming. Here are a few listings of shows that can really bring you down. Will you watch them?

7:00 PM (**2**)THAT'S ALL I NEED RIGHT NOW—News
Isn't it amazing how everything seems to happen at just the wrong time? How can people be so stupid and inconsiderate?

(**3**)I WOULD IF I COULD, BUT I CAN'T—Game Show
Contestants come up with excuses, excuses. They win no prizes or money at all, but it's not their fault.

7:30 (2) WHAT'S WRONG WITH ME?—Medical Game Show
Contestants match their symptoms to those of serious and rare illnesses.

(3) IF YOU REALLY LOVED ME—Soap Opera
Ongoing drama of day-to-day events in your marriage. Your spouse's actions examined in excruciating detail. Tonight: As usual, he or she falls short of *real* love.

8:00 (2) THE ROAD TO RUIN—Business Report
Tonight's feature: What If I'm Fired? Liabilities overtake assets; layoffs are imminent. Special Report: Bankruptcy Looks Like the Only Alternative.

(3) MY NEW CAREER—All-Talk Show
That job you've always wanted and how it's just not the time to make a move.

8:30 (2) COULD IT BE AN AFFAIR?—Marital Mystery
Subtle clues, circumstantial evidence. Naw, it couldn't be . . . But then again. . . . Who says you can't make something out of nothing?

(3) WHAT WILL MAKE ME MAD?—Game Show
Contestants try to avoid saying things that make the boss mad or they're Out the Door. Entire show done on tiptoes.

9:00 (2) THE CORPORATE GONG SHOW—Game Show
Your subordinates are given projects to do without constant directions and guidance from you. Of course, they mess up. Tune in for the hilarious and frightening results.

(3) YOU'VE GOT TO KNOW SOMEBODY—Drama
Weekly stories illustrate the point that opportunities go not to the competent and qualified, but to people who brownnose and play politics. Tonight: Forget Seniority—He Drinks With the Boss.

9:30 (2) LEAVE IT TO MANAGEMENT—Situation Comedy
Bumbling, fumbling, changing requirements twice a day. The fact that these guys never actually learned to do anything doesn't stop them from telling *you* what to do. Tonight: Enough Input, Get Back to Work.

(3) LEAVE IT TO LABOR—Situation Comedy
In late, leaving early, goofing off, fouling up, getting sick. These guys will do anything to avoid an honest day's work. Tonight: Don't Talk to Me about the Work Ethic, I'm on Break.

10:00 (2)THE WRONG DECISION—**Drama**
Panic galore when you realize all those decisions you made today were probably wrong. Tonight: Maybe I Can Buy It Back.

(3)WHAT IF THEY AUDIT?—Sports
Mental gymnastics to explain line items and make them sound legitimate. Tonight: How Big Can a Miscellaneous Category Actually Be?

10:30 (2)I'M SO STRESSED—**News**
Continuous reports on all the things you have to do and the catastrophes that will happen if they are not done.

(3)BACKLOG—**Old News**
Replay of yesterday's listings with special focus on all the things that didn't get done. If you don't work any faster, you'll be completely overwhelmed.

11:00 (2)WHAT DID HE MEAN BY THAT?—**Drama**
Endless obsessing about casual comments and throwaway lines made by people who are important. Tonight: What Did the Chairman *Really* Think about My Report?

(3)I SHOULDA SAID—**Comedy**
All of a sudden, your mind becomes unblocked. Snappy rejoinders and how they might have changed your life.

11:30 (3)THE ACCOUNTING DEPARTMENT IS OUT TO GET ME—
Paranoid Fantasy
No matter what you do, it's wrong. They are out to pin the entire National Deficit on your department. No one can stop them because no one understands what they do.

12:00 (2)ATTACK OF THE IRS—**Horror Movie**
Big Brother ruins lives of upstanding people like you for the sake of mere technicalities. You never know who's next.

(3)GODZILLA IV—**Horror Movie**
Prehistoric monster comes to U.S.A. in shipment of Toyotas. Destroys industry and jobs; buys nothing.

(4)THE GIANT LAWSUIT—**Horror Movie**
Gray-clad attorneys plot to destroy life as we know it.

2:00 AM (2)ALL MY PROBLEMS—**Late Night Drama**
Review of the worst events of yesterday, today and tomorrow. For those who prefer not to sleep.

12

Irritability

Working with a crabby dinosaur can really test your patience. An irritable lizard will bite your head off if you smile at the wrong time, bristle with outrage if you ask a question, or try to drown you in the office water cooler if you're late with a report.

Sometimes the person who's out of sorts might even be you.

Expressing your feelings is important to psychological health, but nobody really benefits from continually expressing irritation. It's unpleasant for you, and it's even worse if you tend to take out these frustrations on your colleagues.

Blowing up or having a tantrum usually involves emotionally over-responding to little things that wouldn't necessarily bother others as much. Reacting in this way can be bad for your career and give you a reputation as a hothead.

Recent studies indicate over-aggressiveness and a tendency to put others on the defensive keep people from achieving their potential as managers more often than any other behavior. People do notice irritability, and it does get in their way. (A peculiar thing I've observed is that some old-line macho businessmen who think women don't make good managers "because they're too emotional" don't consider their own irritability as an emotional response, but rather as the God-given right of males.)

Some businesspeople with irritability problems believe that their outbursts lower their tension level and make it less likely that they will blow up again. This is the fundamental misconception about anger. I call it Freud's "excess gas" theory of emotion. Freud believed that emotions build up in the system like digestive gas and must be released occasionally to get rid of pressure.

Recent research has shown that this theory is not true. Flying off the handle raises your physiological arousal level and keeps it up. It also makes it more likely that you will fly off the handle again, and it leaves others with a reason to get back at you.

How does irritability work? Like other emotional responses, it comes from the Dinosaur Brain, and, with awareness and practice, can be controlled or prevented by recognizing that crabbiness is a four-step process.

1. First, there must be an underlying cause for increased arousal, for instance, stress, worry or low self-esteem. Often the cause of overarousal is chronic. For women, hormonal changes linked to the monthly cycle can create emotional, as well as physical, changes that come under the heading of premenstrual tension. Overuse of caffeine, alcohol or other drugs may also play a big part in setting the stage for an outburst.

2. Next comes an irritating situation, usually not anything very big, that people mistakenly assume is the real cause of their anger.

3. Physiological arousal then becomes higher and more apparent. Usually the heart rate goes up first. Other physical signals include a reddened face, tense muscles, clenched teeth, headache, indigestion or trembling. Many people report a cold feeling in the stomach or down the back.

4. The final step involves thoughts that make the situation worse. They may come out in rational-sounding language, but the words are all Lizard Logic.

Irritable people usually seem to blow up over something they "just can't believe":

"I can't believe she did that when I told her. . . ."

"I just can't believe anybody could be so stupid! How could he make such a dumb mistake? He should know better than that!"

Actually, the Dinosaur Brain is pumping itself up by repeating these unbelievable offenses and justifying the reason for such anger by playing back this dialogue again and again. Instant replay on the old internal TV. Few people blow up without this internal monologue. Sometimes, you can actually hear the irritated person stomping down the office corridor, muttering the lizard's litany aloud: "I just can't believe anybody could be so bird-brained!"

The best way to be in control is to recognize that this internal conversation is a way of arousing yourself rather than an actual explanation of what's going on at work. When you hear your Dinosaur Brain hissing, "I just can't believe . . ." you should ignore it. Sit down. Relax. Blowing up is a luxury most of us cannot afford.

Walt just knew it was going to be one of those days. No cream for his breakfast coffee. And how many times did he have to remind those kids to squeeze the toothpaste from the end of the tube? Then, on the freeway into the city, he was boxed in between a tail-gater and one of those oversized trucks. And now, here comes that jerk from down the hall, whistling that stupid song that would rattle around in Walt's head for the rest of the morning. Walt has half a mind to just nail that guy right now and tell him to keep his dumb birdcalls to himself.

As Walt's irritation rose with every morning mishap, he kept running them over and over. By the time he got to his office, his Dinosaur Brain was so pumped up that it was looking for someone to attack.

The best way to control this kind of pattern is to recognize the Dinosaur Brain's pattern of stringing mishaps together and replaying them. Stop the explosion by stopping the internal grumbling. Snapping a rubber band on his wrist may have reminded Walt that he needed to calm down before he blew.

For most of us it takes practice to recognize the warning signs. We're like Walt in that we don't see the explosion coming until the fuse is lit. We can still save the bacon. Walt's impulse was to spring from his chair and confront the whistler in the corridor. But if Walt gives in to that impulse, he will have lost control at work, had a public tantrum over a triviality, made headlines in the office rumor mill and quite possibly made an enemy of his bewildered and embarrassed colleague.

Now let's take a look at what Walt could do if he switched to cortical thinking before leaving his chair. First, he could take a couple of deep breaths, close his eyes and consciously relax his muscles. (Chapter 18 contains a more complete discussion of stress-relieving techniques.)

Then he could quickly review the morning's low spots, beginning with the creamless coffee for breakfast, and try to spot the real reason for his irritability. Maybe the extra jolt of caffeine set his nerves jangling. Or maybe he woke up feeling stressed because his month-end report was five days late. Maybe the hallway whistler really is a royal pain in the kazoo, but, Walt should ask himself, is the unwanted concert enough of a problem to cause a public blowup?

If he uses his cortex, he has a choice. Most important, he needs to stop repeating the morning's offenses, one after the other, again and again. If he continues, his Dinosaur Brain will have convinced his cortex that this is such a bad day, anything is justified. It's funny how people who do this kind of injustice-and-incredibly-stupid-incident collecting seem to have one bad day after another. Whom the gods wish to destroy, they first make angry—then watch as they destroy themselves.

People who have the habit of internally repeating injustices need to recognize that replaying that program only makes things worse. They need to change the channel. A rubber band on the wrist, snapped when the show starts, can serve as a channel-changing reminder.

Taking a few minutes to calm himself physically and mentally will help Walt shift to rational thinking and away from the Dinosaur Brain's credo: If something is wrong, find people to blame and punish them. As Walt's cortex takes control, he'll realize he really isn't too keen to duke it out with The Whistler, and maybe he'd better skip the coffee and switch to fruit juice for the rest of the morning while he gets to work on that overdue report.

Many women in business face problems as they reach the "glass ceiling " that blocks them from rising to the same professional levels as their male colleagues. At nearly every stage of their careers, women must still deal with unequal standards of professional behavior. One of these certainly has to do with the rules for irritability.

If a male supervisor snaps at his employees, he might be labeled "an aggressive leader." If a woman is curt, she's "a vicious bitch." Irritability hurts everyone, but it hurts women more. Knowing how to control her irritability can be a major step toward a woman's professional success.

Barbara hasn't had a single minute to herself since she woke up. Her alarm didn't go off so, of course, the whole family was late: Nobody would even think of getting up without good old Mom to call them. Then everybody wanted something different for breakfast, and guess who's the family chef? Right. Then there were lunches to pack. Just once, why couldn't they make their own sandwiches? What do they think she is, a slave? Even her husband, standing in the kitchen acting helpless, while she's flying around with a knife globbed with peanut butter, looking for the bread. Men.

There was no time for her own breakfast. No way. Not unless she decided to go to the office in her nightgown. Her skirt was too tight at the waistband; her stomach felt fat; her head was splitting and her hands shook as she drove to work. Her period was due any day, and her body felt ready to explode.

Barbara just couldn't believe how lousy this day was already. Her phone was ringing as she sat down at her desk, and it didn't stop all morning. If that weren't bad enough, people kept walking by and dropping papers onto her desk. Urgent. ASAP. Everybody wanted her attention right now. Why couldn't they just leave her alone for two minutes? Don't they know she's just one person? She can't even think straight. The next person who even looks at her cross-eyed is really gonna get it.

Barbara's irritability is caused by an overloaded schedule, both at home and at work, and made worse by the physical and emotional symptoms of premenstrual tension. Instead of biting off the head of the next colleague who passes her desk, there are ways Barbara can calm herself and switch from her Dinosaur Brain to rational thinking.

Like Walt, Barbara needs to stop the running account of injustices in her head and slow down her physical responses, by breathing deeply and relaxing her muscles. If she can't do this while sitting at her desk, a quick trip to the privacy of the women's room would be well worth the time.

She may want to gain further distance from her irritated feelings. Taking a quick walk down the corridor or going to the office lunchroom for a cup of yogurt and two headache tablets would remove her from the scene of her frustration and give her a chance to get her feelings under control before she faces the thundering herd again. (Eating the yogurt—and not a sugar doughnut—will also give her some lasting energy and might help ease her headache. We all are more likely to behave like dinosaurs when we're hungry.)

Barbara also needs to do more long-term planning. Unlike Walt's irritation with the office whistler, Barbara's frustrations are more permanent. Her schedule is typical of the many businesswomen who juggle full-time jobs and full-time family duties.

She needs to take an hour for herself and examine her life. Her irritated question of the morning, "What does her family think she is, a slave?" is a good one to ask herself when she is feeling calmer. Does she feel she needs to be a slave or a superwoman? If the answer is still yes, Barbara and her family need to sit down and work out a more equal arrangement of domestic duties. For starters, everybody really could make his or her own lunch every day.

She will have to ask for what she wants, and sometimes she may have to let her husband and the kids go off without lunch. If she doesn't, she'll be back in chains in no time.

If Barbara's irritability and physical symptoms occur in a monthly pattern that she can predict and anticipate, she must be very aware of her calendar. During her times of high irritability, she must be particularly careful to think before she snaps at someone.

It would also be helpful for her to see a doctor and discuss her medical options. While current opinions differ about successful treatment for symptoms of the premenstrual syndrome, regular exercise and a healthy diet show up on most physicians' recommended lists.

Many business people take drinks or drugs to relax them. The effects the next day or day after that are anything but relaxing. Any drug —alcohol, cocaine, tranquilizers, pot—depletes brain chemicals that can inhibit aggressive responses. Often people don't realize that their arousal is caused by the chemical substance they drank, smoked or snorted a few days ago. They think the drug has cleared their system. It hasn't. The effects of marijuana especially may last up to a week.

The key for anyone who has trouble with irritability on the job is to remember that blowing up over little things doesn't do anyone any good and often does some harm. The best time to stop these outbursts is before they happen.

(P.S. If someone anonymously leaves this chapter open on your desk, don't get angry. Ask other colleagues if they think there's room for change in your I.Q. (Irritability Quotient). And remember what my grandfather used to say: "If three people call you a horse, buy a saddle!")

13

Manipulation

Manipulation is a dirty word. When we talk about it, we describe bending people to our will, twisting words, pressuring people, screwing people over. When you think about how it feels to be manipulated—that wrenching, tight feeling in your stomach—it's not surprising that we use this kind of imagery.

We know how it feels, but what is it? Manipulation quite simply involves maneuvering you into your Dinosaur Brain, then using its predictability and limited response patterns to control you when you don't want to be controlled.

Nearly all manipulators use one of the following strategies:

Intimidation and the Emotional Scene. The unwritten rule these manipulators play by is that they are so obnoxious, you'll give them their way to get rid of them. You often see this technique in restaurants, when a blustering lizard threatens and complains until the headwaiter gives him or her a table just to stop the bully from disturbing other diners. This kind of intimidation also happens at the office.

Roger's theory of management is that a quiet staff is a happy staff. He has team meetings at which issues are discussed, but everybody knows they risk his ridicule and anger if they make any critical comments. Roger says, "My door is always open," and it is if you want to talk about football, but if you have any criticism about him or the way he does business, it's easy to make his hit list.

When people do mention a problem, usually long after it's passed, Roger always says, "Why didn't you bring it up then? Let's just have a rule that if you don't talk about it at the time, you can't bring it up later."

Working for someone like Roger involves a great deal of mixed feelings. Should you mention a problem and provoke his wrath or let him manipulate you into keeping quiet, thus delegating his stress to you?

Roger acts like a dominant lizard and regards any criticism as a threat to his rule. He manipulates by intimidation and puts everybody into the flight or fright response. How do you deal with such a person?

Break the silence. You can start by raising criticism in an oblique way. Ask questions, such as "How do you think this will go over with the people in production?" Instead of saying what's wrong, you might suggest an alternative course of action: "Another way we could do that, which wouldn't get the production guys up in arms, is. . . ." This implies that you are not taking production's side against Roger.

Accept ridicule. If you don't get into your Dinosaur Brain, the manipulator will be the one who'll look bad. If you're attacked in a meeting, just stand there looking him or her straight in the eyes and make no effort to defend yourself. If you do that, the manipulator will get further and further into his or her Dinosaur Brain, and you will have turned the tables.

If you work for someone like this, you'll have to accept ridicule sometime. Managers like Roger always say they want people who'll stand up to them, but I've never known this to be true. If you're going to be fired for criticizing, it's probably better to get it over with. Nobody needs that kind of job.

The fear of being fired is worse, psychologically, than actually being fired. If you're fired, you can mourn, learn from it and get over it. If you live in fear of being fired, you continually limit your actions and speech and often have to compromise your principles. You die the "little death," as Hemingway said, every day. Actually, it's not all that easy to fire somebody. You might as well find out what the limits are rather than go on living in fear.

Don't get reinforcements. A dinosaur whose subordinates have gone over his or her head is the most dangerous lizard in the corporate jungle. Unless you think you can get the manipulator fired, you have to deal with this problem by yourself. Getting a group of people together to sign a petition against the person will do you no good. The manipulator will just try to separate you, or single out one particular person (probably you) as the messenger who gets beheaded. If you go to his or her boss, it's usually a wasted effort because the person he or she reports to often won't care that the staff is upset. The boss cares about whether the manipulator is accomplishing his or her goals and objectives.

The only successful way to beat somebody like this is either to leave or to reach the point where you aren't afraid of being yelled at.

The second part of this category involves manipulation by excessive emotion. If you're willing to endure a few tears or some yelling, you're a long way ahead. These people rely on your mistaken belief that it takes less time and is easier just to give them what they want, instead of standing up to them and settling the situation. This may be true in the short run, but if they can get away with it once, they'll do it again.

Carol is a casualty. She comes to your office about once a week, stressed out or bummed out over something. It might be the buzzing of the lights in her work area, smoke in the air, problems at home—some reason why she can't do exactly what is expected of her.

Your usual pattern is to give her a sick day and ease up on her deadlines just to get rid of her. Very soon you begin to notice that she operates under a different set of rules from everybody else in your department. Inside her head, Carol thinks, "I just can't take it. This is overwhelming me. Somebody has to help because I certainly can't do it." She feels fragile and weak. To you, she may seem like a burden or someone who maneuvers you into feeling an obligation for her.

Typically people like Carol are quite skilled at letting you know that you're their only hope. Here's what to do with such a person:

First and foremost, don't change the rules. When you let a manipulator know that emotional outbursts are rewarded with changes in job descriptions, you've lost.

If the person is really handicapped, he or she will require accommodation, but the rules should be spelled out clearly as an adjunct to his or her job description. Accommodations are a contract with the employer and should be handled as such.

Learn to tolerate the tears or the yelling. Realize that just because she's frantic, you don't necessarily have to be. Ignore the emotion and stay focused on the problem.

Set a time limit before you start talking to her. Some people, like Carol, want action, but many just want to be listened to and soothed for at least 45 minutes twice a week. Realize that the ones who want action are the harder to deal with, but maybe if you listen, the ones who want action will feel satisfied enough so that you won't have to change things for them.

Say something like, "I'm willing to talk to you about this, but I have five minutes. I will listen to you, but at the end of five minutes, I'm going to stop to make a phone call" (or go down to purchasing, or whatever.) "Is that OK?" Once you have a verbal contract, it will be easier for you to hold to it.

Many times these employees who need something are good at their jobs and are worth keeping. Five minutes twice a week is a good investment. (If the person asks for more time, it's OK to say no or to set an appointment for three days later.)

People like Carol operate on turning their emergency into your emergency. If they can't do that, they calm down more easily and feel better, more in control. Calm is contagious.

Managers often tend to get rid of someone like this because he or she is emotionally draining. If you follow a schedule and allow the person to vent, you won't feel drained and you may be rewarded with an employee who feels understood.

Always find out what she wants to happen or what she wants you to do. Manipulative behaviors very seldom involve directly asking for something. Manipulators hint at it; they try to get you to guess or to keep working until you do the right thing. If they tell you directly what they want you to do, you can then say no, and the game is over.

Asking "What do you want me to do?" is particularly effective with manipulators of all sorts because you can use their answer as a basis for negotiating. Of course, this technique also makes them stop and think, which may activate their cortex.

If more than five minutes twice a week is needed, direct the manipulator to the people who can really help him or her. Doing therapy is not part of your job, but that of a family doctor, your Employee Assistance Program representative, a psychologist or whomever might be an appropriate source of referral.

Set up the situation so that the manipulator has to work harder to complain to you, rather than having you take some responsibility away. You turn the tables. Every time the manipulator comes to you, make him or her do something.

For example, say, "This sounds serious. You need to make an appointment with your doctor (or Employee Assistance person) today and have him or her give me a call so we can decide what to do." Or you could have the manipulator do a survey on people's perceptions of smoke in their area and write a report about it. If the manipulator has to do more to complain than to keep quiet, he or she is much more likely to be silent.

Trying to Make You Look Bad. Everything depends on your credibility within the group. If somebody gets you to blow up or act like a lizard, everyone will remember the time you really lost it long after they've forgotten the issue itself. In the long run, victory always goes to the coolest. Manipulators are very good at pushing you into your Dinosaur Brain so that you start acting emotionally at just the wrong time.

Larry was a systems analyst for Dinocorp. His job involved analyzing a division's work flow and devising a plan for the division head for more efficient and effective operation. Larry's goal was to be the CEO's fair-haired boy. He had a lot of training but little ability or desire to consider things in depth. He would come in, very quickly look over an operation and make some arbitrary decisions about how the company should be run.

Then he would call a meeting to present his plan, which invariably contained major and unreasonable changes in the way the managers had to do their jobs. They in turn would start protesting and get angry. Although Larry provoked them in subtle ways, it would seem to the division head and the CEO that the managers were a bunch of fuddy-duddies, attacking Larry because he had come up with new ideas. Larry would stay cool, look at the boss and shrug his shoulders as the managers yelled and screamed.

The fact that Larry's ideas weren't well conceived and that he hadn't done the necessary sales job on the plan was lost in the Godzilla-meets-Rodan effect. Larry made himself look good by being cool and calm and sticking to the facts while everybody else was yelling at him.

Eventually one of the managers had had enough. The next time Larry submitted a proposal, this manager insisted that everyone hold off on his or her criticism until Larry had finished. Then the manager fired off a series of questions, beginning with, "Well, you've decided to recommend this plan. What are some of the other ideas that you came up with and discarded?" Larry hemmed and hawed until it became clear that he was shooting from the hip. He hadn't considered any other ideas.

The older manager then asked about the reactions of certain customers and suppliers to segments of his plan. When Larry said he couldn't exactly remember talking with those people, the manager pinned him down with more names and asked if he could remember talking to any of them. "Well, no, I can't," Larry finally said.

"That's pretty interesting," the manager replied. "I have some other questions too." Within ten minutes, he had demonstrated to all exactly how Larry had done his job.

Larry had discovered that he could get just as far with the boss by manipulating people into attacking him as by doing careful work. When he was the victim of an unprovoked attack, he looked like the only rational guy in the room. Attention shifted away from the quality or feasibility of his plan and toward the emotions of the managers. Even if the plan failed later, Larry could always say it would have worked if the other guys had "gone along with the program." Using your Dinosaur Brain can sometimes save people a lot of work.

When the older manager focused on Larry's work rationally, he could tear it apart in a way that wouldn't have been possible if he were yelling.

Making people look bad is also a favorite technique of interviewers and cross-examiners. In the beginning they try to elicit as much information as possible then later attack your consistency. They'll use your words out of context, purposely misunderstand, twist what you say and misquote you. Their goal is to ask you the kind of question—the classic is, "Have you stopped beating your wife?"— in which, no matter what you answer, you end up looking bad.

What do you do in this situation?

Stay cool. Talk slowly. Take all the time you need to stop and think. If the manipulator is an impulsive person, your stopping to think will be infuriating, and he or she will go into Dinosaur Brain behavior, which will make you look better.

Give no more information than is needed. Answer only the question asked. Unless you need to give specific information, be vague.

Manipulators need some information about your feelings or behaviors in order to gain control over you. The less they have, the less harm they can do. They rely on the fact that, if they just sound interested, you'll spill your guts and give them plenty of material to work with. If you don't do that, they might ask you more pointed questions, thus giving their strategy away and putting you in a position where you can ask, "Why do you need to know that?"

Ask questions—but not the kind that give your position away as this one does: "You didn't run this by any customers, did you?" In general, with information, it's better to receive than to give.

Pay attention to the process. In any conversation, there is always process and content. Content is what is said; process is the way it is said. When you're dealing with manipulators, think about what they are trying to do and how they are going about it rather than what they are actually saying. They count on the fact that you will focus on the details while they sneak around and take you from the rear.

Most important, remember no law says you have to answer every question that's asked of you. Manipulators rely on your sense of courtesy. They know most people will answer questions because it is considered polite. However, it is always permissible not to answer and to ask why the manipulator wants to know that. Just remember to keep your voice calm and your tone courteous.

For example, you can smile and say, "You want to know if I stopped beating my wife. Well, you've got me there. You've maneuvered me into a position where, if I answer yes, I look bad, and if I say no, I still look bad. I don't see how I can answer a question like that at all."

The Implied Debt. Some manipulators know that if you both are part of the same herd, you can't ignore a distress call. Their strategy involves sending out strong loyalty-and-affiliation cues. Then, when you feel as if your relationship is close, they send out the distress call. If you say yes, you feel a bit used. If you say no, the manipulator looks at you in a way that makes you feel like slime.

Frieda is so nice and caring. "Motherly" is the word that comes to mind. She always sends a card on your birthday, or little gifts now and then; she always has kind words and lunches. Everything she says and does lets you know you are very important to her. She is such a nice person that you just can't turn her down when she asks you to work overtime for the third time this week or to defer on that raise because the department is so poor. Frieda pulls the same thing on her boss. If you tell her no, she can even generate a little tear at the corner of her eye.

It's not that Frieda is faking anything. She believes that if you're nice to people, they'll be nice to you. Frieda regards this convention as natural law. She knows at some level that her gifts and lunches are a good investment, and most often they're of less value than what she gets you to do in return.

The motherly Frieda in this example could just as well be cute Kitty, the office's kid sister, or boyish Neal, the department's whiz kid. They all use the implied-debt form of manipulation to get what they want. How do you deal with people like this?

Play their game. Return their gifts in kind instead of doing extra work for them. Whenever they give you something, give them something back, so there is never an outstanding debt. This may get them to shift into overdrive, and if they do, get some verbal agreement that if you accept their latest round of kindnesses, it doesn't obligate you. Of course they'll agree, and you can save that assurance for later when they ask you to do something you don't want to do.

Don't be afraid to say no. Recognize that these manipulators are perfectly capable of taking care of themselves and won't fall apart if you don't do what they want. Realize too that if their approval is contingent on your doing everything they want, you'll always be displeasing them in some way. It's best that it be out in the open and that it be now.

How many Friedas does it take to change a lightbulb? "None, dear, I'll just sit here in the dark." With someone like this, you have to be able to say no and let her do her worst.

The Attack from the Blind Side. Manipulation always comes indirectly. It hits you from the side where you are most vulnerable.

Samuel B. White has been CEO of Lizards Inc. for the last eleven years. It's a large company with many divisions, and he takes a personal interest in each when the mood strikes him. It's well known that he can make or break any career, so up-and-coming executives are thrilled when Sam invites them to one of his intimate dinner parties.

They are plied with drinks from the minute they arrive. After dinner, over coffee, brandy and cigars, old Sam will often start conversations and share his opinions about different parts of the company, people they know, his ideas about the future and where a particular young executive might fit in. They continue to drink and, since Sam has a pretty hefty tolerance, usually the younger men's tongues get looser and looser.

Sam: "You know, Jerry, for a long time I've thought Bill Schwartz, your division head, is getting a little bit rusty. Some of the decisions he's made leave something to be desired. Like the Baldwin contract, for instance. . . ."

Jerry: "Yes, sir, I think that too. And not only that, a lot of the younger guys in the department feel like he's kind of holding us down, you know. There are a lot of new things we could do, but Bill doesn't want anybody to do anything unless he gets the credit for it."

Sam: "Hmmmmm, that's interesting. Can you give me any example of that?"

Jerry: "I sure can. You know that idea about stocking fewer inventories at the plants and instead ordering things when we need them? Well, that was my idea and he took the credit for it."

Sam: "Well, we'll have to do something about that, Jerry."

Jerry, the young executive, mistook the situation. He thought Sam was treating him as a peer, sharing intimacies. Only later did he find out that what he said had been used against him, and the promises old Sam made were forgotten the next day.

What Sam actually ended up doing was telling the division head that one of his younger guys does a lot of talking about him. Good old Sam.

This sort of manipulation consolidates the power at the top. It also tends to undermine the chain of command, but Sam is the top dinosaur, and this is one of the ways he stays on top.

It's a mistake to try to get manipulators to acknowledge their agendas. If you say, "What you're really trying to do is make me . . . ," they'll deny it.

Here are some better ways to deal with a hidden agenda:

Know your limit regarding alcohol.

Ask yourself, Why is he asking me that?

Remember that gossiping is always a temptation, and don't give in to temptation. When you're talking to the boss, if you can't say anything nice about someone, don't say anything. Pretend the other person is in the room and phrase your comments accordingly.

If you need to run off at the mouth,

Praise co-workers

Talk about how great a particular idea is

Criticize somebody who's gone

Share your plans for the future

Ask old Sam about the good old days. (This often distracts old dinosaurs: They can't resist telling their stories.)

Remember that only liars swear they're telling the truth. People who are telling the truth assume they'll be believed; they don't even think of swearing. When people say, "You can be candid with me," beware!

Sometimes someone you supervise will try to manipulate you by appealing to your vulnerable side, for instance, your sense of compassion. When you recognize this as a tactic, you can use your cortex to focus on the real issue. You can say, for example, "Well, we can continue this, but I just want you to know that I'm absolutely unwilling to change the date that your report is due. We can talk some more about your grandmother's illness, if you like, but I want it to be clear between us that the due date still stands."

Manipulators will then almost invariably change the subject by asking a question. They expect that you'll be drawn into the next topic, and they can move around to what they want in a different way. Remember, you don't have to answer a question. You can always say, "All right, I'm willing to answer that question, but first I want to be very clear that I'm not going to change the due date."

Often they'll act as if they didn't even hear you. You may have to get some verbal acknowledgement that they heard what you said before you move on. If you do that, usually the manipulation dries up and blows away, once the lizards realize they can't get what they want.

None of the types of manipulation discussed in this chapter can work unless you are reacting with your Dinosaur Brain. People don't take advantage of someone who's thinking. It's important to recognize the gut-wrenching feelings that say, "Somebody's trying to manipulate me" as a signal to stay cool and let those feelings pass before you take action. You must be able to see clearly what's going on before you do anything.

Decide what you want and make your behavior reflect your goal instead of the manipulator's. Don't be afraid to avoid answering questions, if the questions are used as manipulation or diversion tactics.

You must also be willing to have people be angry with you, because if manipulators can't beat you, they will get mad. If you can avoid reacting with your Dinosaur Brain, their anger can just slide off your back.

14

The Positive Uses
of Anger

Having read this book to this point, you might be thinking, "This guy is totally against anger. He doesn't think it can ever be positive." Yet, in your experience, there have been many times when anger has been positive.

I agree. I'm not taking a stand against anger itself; I am against anger as a management style. Anger can be a powerful form of direct communication or a person's usual way of interacting with the world. It cannot be both.

There are certainly times when anger can be valuable personally and in relationships with colleagues. Let's look at some situations in which anger can be positive.

Personal Expression. Carl is the purchasing agent for XYZ Inc. He's usually an easy-going guy who takes his job seriously and wants to do his best for the company. For years Carl has been buying office supplies from Ed's Discount Office Supplies, and Ed has always assured him that he's getting the very best price, the same as the big corporate customers pay. (Carl's company is on the small side.)

By chance, Carl discovered that some of Ed's other customers were paying considerably less for computer paper than he was being charged and that Ed had been stringing him along all these years. Carl was really ticked.

Of course, he was going to stop doing business with Ed. He could have just canceled his order, but Carl felt that he wouldn't be being true to himself if he didn't pick up the phone and tell Ed what he thought of his shoddy business practices. So Carl called Ed and chewed him out, which made him feel as if the situation were fully settled. He still thinks Ed is a creep, but he's not holding a grudge.

In this case, anger was a way for Carl to express his feelings. He handled the situation effectively and was true to his own emotions. His anger was positive.

Emphasis. *Kris knew Shannon was goofing off. Kris had stuck out her neck to hire her because she thought Shannon really had what it takes. Shannon had made all kinds of promises about how hard she would work, but she had been late on several reports and what she had turned in was a half-baked effort.*

Kris realized this was a performance problem, but she also felt cheated because Shannon wasn't coming through on the promises she had made. Kris could have handled the situation on a case-by-case basis, but instead she decided to call Shannon and tell her in no uncertain terms how she felt.

This definitely was not Kris's typically supportive, positive way of dealing with Shannon. When Shannon heard how angry Kris was, she began to think about her own behavior.

When used sparingly, anger can demonstrate to other people the importance of your feelings.

Motivation. *Elaine is good at her job, and she knows it, but she feels that her boss quite consistently undervalues her and doesn't use her to her full potential. He has made little comments here and there, and he seems to walk her through tasks more than he does others. It had begun to irritate her, but Elaine had decided to keep quiet and just do the best job she could, until the Dawson project came up.*

She went to her boss and said, "I want the Dawson assignment. I can do it." He looked at her, looked down and mumbled something about Joe's being a bit more experienced. At that point, Elaine decided it was now or never. She slammed her hand down on the desk and said, "No! I won't hear about Joe doing it! You need to give me a chance. I can do this project! You're undervaluing me, and I want a chance to show you how good I really am!"

The boss nearly jumped out of his chair. Then he said, "Well if you feel that strongly about it, take it and see if you can run with it."

Elaine's anger was building up. She knew what was bothering her, but her anger had to reach a certain point before it motivated her to take the big step and defy her boss and demand that he let her take the project.

Opening Closed Communication. *Frank and Maggie are the heads of accounting and personnel, respectively. For months they seemed to have been at odds on every issue, sniping away until their mutual animosity was getting in the way of communication between their departments. Finally they decided they needed to get things out in the open and air them.*

Maggie and Frank went into her office, closed the door and had a knock-down, drag-out fight, bringing up all their thorny issues, personal as well as professional. In the end, they didn't like each other any better, but they had agreed to disagree and had found a method of getting their personal feelings out of the way so that they could go back to doing their jobs.

Being directly angry at someone can be a sign of respect. We can't always like everybody else, and sometimes we have to do the other person the favor of being direct about our feelings. If people at the same professional level get a chance to air their personality clashes occasionally in a way both find acceptable, the process sometimes can take a lot of the strain off the relationship.

Dynamite. *Zach was sick and tired of the same old bull. This was the fourth meeting on whether the company was going to spend the bucks to market the new product. The marketing surveys were in, and they looked* *good. Engineering had a good design, but nobody was clearly coming out on spending all that money. This meeting, like every other, was becoming an exercise in bureaucratic tail-covering. Zach knew it would end like the other three, with somebody calling for some new piece of obscure information that was needed before a decision could be made. He decided he wasn't going to tolerate it any more.*

Zach stood up, knocking over his chair, and said, "I'm sick and tired of this. All we're doing is sitting here covering our tails and not making a decision. We're paid to be managers, and we're supposed to decide things, even difficult things, instead of putting them off into the future. If all we're going to do is figure out some other little bit of unknown data, I'm going back to my office. I've got some real work to do." He then stormed out.

Needless to say, Zach got everybody's attention. If he had displayed this kind of anger regularly, nobody would have taken any notice, but Zach had a reputation for being a level-headed guy. This explosion really made people think, and Zach was able to dynamite the logjam and get the project moving again.

How can you tell if your anger is a positive force? This area is very subjective. Some people think their anger is a positive force because it's productive; it gets them what they want. The problem with this is that, while it may well get them what they want, it comes at the cost of credibility and respect from colleagues. If you're abrasive and explosive, nobody will come up to you and tell you about it, because they're afraid you'll blow up. You're going to have to consider your own anger and decide for yourself.

Decisions about whether your anger is a positive force may be based on:

Frequency. Anybody can blow up once in a while, but there is a big difference between someone who blows up twice a year and one who erupts twice a day. There is no saying what the dividing line is, but if you lose your temper less than once a month (I mean really lose it, not just an expletive deleted here and there), you're probably within the normal range.

Focus. When you get angry, do you know why or at what? Some people are mad at the world most of the time and dump their rage on the first poor soul who makes a mistake.

Proportion. Is the amount of anger you're expressing appropriate to the situation, or are you blowing a little thing way out of proportion?

Direction. Are you yelling at the person who really makes you angry, or are you griping about someone behind his or her back or running on about the injustices you've suffered at the hand of someone you're afraid to confront?

Repetition. Are you saying something that you feel and getting it out of your system, or are you repeating the story over and over and fanning your own flame?

Duration. When you're angry, do you express it and then it's over, or do you bear a grudge for a long time?

Style. When you're angry, do you tell about what's bothering you and what you feel, rather than what's wrong with the other person? Do you indulge in name-calling? I have never seen a positive use for name-calling.

Audience. Do you express your anger privately to the people at whom it's directed, or do you like to indulge in public humiliation?

Time Orientation. Do you express anger at something that has just happened, or do you rehash the entire relationship every time you blow up? People who say things like "You always" or "You never" tend to let their anger carry excess baggage that is not helpful. Try to express your anger as closely as possible to the event that made you angry.

Reciprocity. Do you yell at people who are free to yell back at you? Do you accept the fact that people are going to get angry at your anger—and do you allow it?—or do your employees, your children and your dog have to bear the brunt of your wrath? Pick on someone your own size.

Evidence. When you get angry, is it at what other people actually do or say, or do you indulge in mind-reading? Mind-reading happens when you get angry at what you think other people's actions mean or at what you think they're thinking. In general, the further you stray from what someone actually did, the less positive your anger will be.

Controllability. When you're angry, do you stop and think for a second or two about whether you can express it and how you'll do it, or do you jump in, no matter who is there? Once you start to explode, can you stop it, or does it have to reach its own conclusion? Do you find yourself going overboard and then having to apologize?

These are guidelines for you to consider. Obviously, no anger is pure and perfect. Sometimes it comes out, and it's not as elegant as we would wish. It can still be a positive force, but only if it doesn't happen too often.

How do you know how often you get angry? You can keep records about it, but probably the best way is to check it out with three friends. Give them permission to tell you what they really think without your blowing up at them. If they say your anger is a problem, maybe you'd like to read this chapter again.

15

Angry Clients

One angry client can spoil your whole day. No matter how courteous and conscientious you are at work, someday you'll have to face someone who is foot-stomping angry at you or your company. What do you do then?

First, it's important to remember that people who are angry cannot reason. If they are extremely angry, they're not using their cortex at all but are relying instead on the primitive emotions based in the Dinosaur Brain.

It's a mistake to treat angry clients as if they had good sense and were capable of normal, logical thought. When people are angry, they make far different responses from when they're coolly evaluating a situation or trying to figure out a solution.

Of course, you can tell that a client is angry when he or she stalks into your office, shouting, shaking a fist and glaring at you. You can hear his or her anger over the telephone if the voice is loud, or mimicking and sarcastic. Anybody can see and hear anger at this point. The more visibly angry someone is, the less likely he or she will be to respond rationally.

Most people start getting angry before they realize it and can signal their feelings in more subtle and unconscious ways. If you're face to face with an angry client, you can see this happening if the client suddenly stiffens, draws deeper and more deliberate breaths, clenches his jaw or taps her foot or fingers. Sentences may get shorter or more curt. Your client might glance at his watch or invade your territory by moving a little too close for comfort. Look also for coloring in the face and neck.

You can even learn to recognize some of the same nonverbal cues in yourself before your own anger level rises and you find yourself wanting to shout back.

It's hard to pinpoint exactly when anger becomes conscious. In business, the rule should be, "As soon as you see any signs, it's time to make some effort to cool things down." Over the years I've developed procedures for coping with angry clients, or colleagues, for that matter, quickly and efficiently. While following these rules won't do away with the problem of angry clients, they will show you how to handle them with the least possible conflict. You'll also find these suggestions can work as well in dealing with enraged supervisors, colleagues and employees. Each is designed to help people move away from the Dinosaur Brain's "anger areas" to the problem-solving areas of the cortex.

Let's start by identifying four techniques that *will not* work. All four will make the client angrier, no matter what else you do or say. They are:

Fighting back
Running away
Explaining
Operating with mixed goals

Fighting Back. When somebody starts yelling at you, a natural response is to want to shout right back. This defense comes from the Dinosaur Brain's internal programming, which says, "If people are angry, show them that *they* are wrong and *I* am right." What usually happens is that, if you fight back, the client will fight harder. Even if this strategy works and you succeed in outshouting him or her, you still lose a customer.

When you're confronted by a client that you want to keep, your goal should be to calm him or her down to the point where you both can work successfully on solving the problem. You'll probably be able to think of hundreds of snappy comebacks and subtle put-downs as the two of you start communicating. But your job will be much easier if you stifle your Dinosaur Brain and keep these responses to yourself, including rolling your eyes and snorting.

Running Away. Telling the client who is really to blame will only bring more anger. Clients think they're getting the runaround. They're right.

Another destructive response that can happen when you're confronted by an angry client is to let your mental faculties blank out. You feel tongue-tied and confused, too overwhelmed by the criticism to answer it logically. It can seem easier just to back down and run away, either by giving in to the client's demands without evaluating them on their merits or by passing the buck to the nearest available colleague. In either case, the client will notice and remember your weakness.

A better choice is to take the time to think about what you will do before you do it. You don't have to respond immediately or answer every question as soon as it's asked.

A client won't be offended if you say, "Wait a minute; I'd like to think about this." Not only are you showing your client, by example, the way you want him or her to behave, but you're also demonstrating that you take the situation seriously.

Explaining. A client's anger is often the result of a simple misunderstanding. It's very tempting for you to rush in and explain what went wrong, but an angry person will often perceive this explanation as an attack and fight back even harder. If a client is yelling, he or she is clearly reacting with the Dinosaur Brain and won't be able to listen to you or deal with what you're saying. Your first step must be to calm the client's anger.

Another reason to avoid explaining is that, in most cases, the client doesn't really care how or why the problem occurred. He or she just wants to see it corrected. At best, explanations serve your needs instead of the customer's. At worst, explaining is far too often a disguised form of fighting back or running away.

Explanations that shift the blame, such as "It's company policy," or "I don't make the rules," are nearly certain to enrage your client further. They don't respond to the client's specific problem and make you sound more interested in passing the buck than in being helpful.

Mixed Goals. The final technique that won't work is having mixed goals. The basic goal that I advocate for dealing with angry clients is to calm them as quickly as possible so that you can help solve their problem rationally. This goal is totally different from "getting back at them." You cannot "get back" at the client and calm him or her at the same time.

Before you deal with an angry client, you need to decide on your goal. If it's to calm the customer down, you have to forget about counterattacking. If at any time you give in to the Dinosaur Brain impulse to add a little dig of your own, you can be sure that the client will respond to that rather than any constructive point you were also trying to make. Avoid acerbic or sarcastic comments of your own, no matter how adept or appropriate your Dinosaur Brain tells you they would be.

Now let's look at techniques that *will* work when you're confronted by an angry client.

Listen and Let the Client Know You Are Listening. Sometimes a client will raise a fuss because he or she thinks it's the only way to be heard. The best way to calm someone like this down is by listening, and do it actively, so that the client knows you are paying attention.

Some effective responses, besides the classic "uh-huh," include:

"That *is* quite a problem."
"I can see how you would be upset about that."
"That would concern me too."

As the client becomes more specific, you can listen actively by re-stating the problem, paraphrasing. This technique is probably the most effective suggestion ever devised for getting along with others. An example of paraphrasing:

Client: I have a copy of my statement right here, and, as far as I'm concerned, the whole damn thing is a mistake.

You: Are you saying that some of those charges are incorrect, Mr. Jones?

Client: I just want to know what gives you the right to charge prices like that!

You: You're concerned about the rate of the charges, is that correct? They seem high to you?

Client: Damn right, they're high. How the hell can you guys charge $150 an hour? I couldn't believe it when I got the bill.

You: Well, I can answer that question for you, Mr. Jones, but first I want to make sure that I understand your concern. I'm sorry that you think the charges are so high, but do you also feel that they're incorrect?

Client (muttering): They're just too damn high.

You: Well, I'm surely sorry that you feel that way. I have a copy of your statement right here, and I'll be happy to go over each charge individually, but I don't think I can change them for you. Would you like me to go through them with you?

Client: No, don't bother. I just think they're awfully high.

In this example, the client isn't completely satisfied with the out-come, but the service rep has maintained control, paraphrased the customer's complaint and, most of all, managed to avoid responding angrily. By the end of the conversation, you'll notice that the client has stopped swearing, a signal that he has begun the switch from the Dinosaur Brain to the cortex.

Find Out What the Client Wants. When you have successfully con-vinced the client that you hear what he or she is saying, you need to find out specifically what is expected from you. The best way to do this is by asking, "What would you like me to do?"

There are several reasons for asking this simple question. First, asking lets you find out exactly what the client wants. Sometimes, especially in the calming-down stage of a discussion, this is not at all clear. Second, and more important, asking this question causes the client to stop and think, thus switching reactions from the Dinosaur Brain to the cortex and automatically toning down his or her emotional response.

Offer Alternatives and Negotiate. Once you find out what the client wants, you can begin to decide what you can do to remedy the situation. You may be surprised how easy this will be if the client feels that he or she has really been heard.

Save Your Client's Face. No one likes to admit that he or she was wrong. The Dinosaur Brain would rather memorize *Robert's Rules of Order* than concede it has made a mistake. In dealing with angry clients it's important to structure the situation so they don't have to admit publicly to you that they were in error. Here are two examples:

> "Well, here's the problem. These two columns weren't added together. Our form is confusing, I know. I've done the same thing myself."

or

> "I'd be just as upset if I thought I wasn't being listened to."

If you can resolve the situation so that the client still feels intelligent, moral and worthwhile, the customer is likely to return.

If the error was clearly yours, say so graciously, apologize for the client's inconvenience, acknowledge his or her right to feel upset and fix the mistake. If the mistake cost the client in time or money, a small discount would be good business. You can turn an angry client into one who feels understood and grateful.

16

The Customer Service Model

We've seen that the Dinosaur Brain has some very explicit ideas about how companies should be organized and run. Whoever is at the top has all the rights and gets all the goodies. The people at the bottom have to do what the head dinosaur says if they want to stay in the herd.

Obviously, this is no way to run a railroad, yet we are all programmed with the belief, somewhere deep in our Dinosaur Brains, that this is how things should be. I think this is what Lord Acton meant when he said, "Power tends to corrupt, and absolute power corrupts absolutely."

In this book so far we've discussed how to exist in systems that are overly influenced by the Dinosaur Brain. This chapter describes a structural model that can prevent some of the worst of the Dinosaur Brain abuses. It's a new idea called the *Customer Service Model* that is being pioneered by several forward-looking companies. It's based on the philosophy that customer service is the most important function that goes on in a company.

In the traditional sense, everybody believes in serving the *customers.* But this model goes a step further in assuming that everyone in the company, not just the people who work at the counter, provides service to customers.

A company that sees customer service as important for all of its employees will almost always have the most productive and psychologically healthy work environment. It defines its customers not only as people from the outside but also as those within the organization.

If you're a manager, for example, you're providing a service—management—to the people you manage and to the executives for whom you manage. Success in your job depends on how well you are meeting the needs of the people you're serving—your customers—just as surely as it does for the guys down in sales.

This raises a question. How do you know how well you're pleasing your customers? Some businesses have found it most instructive to have customer satisfaction ratings for everyone, all the way up to the CEO. People who are managed rate their satisfaction with the people who manage them. Employees in one department who use the services of another rate the responsivity and quality of the services they use.

You are probably reading this and thinking, "Good grief, not more review forms." I can sympathize with that, because in most companies there are about five times as many ratings going on as are needed. The real question is the purpose of the rating. Ratings that are used for something other than legal protection have a place.

There is a place for finding out in an organized way what employees feel they need in order to do their jobs better. What determines whether a system such as this succeeds or fails is how well the people at the top accept and follow it. If one person is above the ratings, the system might as well be scrapped.

Why should top management follow a customer service model? More money and fewer hassles. The conflict between labor and management costs American industry untold billions of dollars a year. This conflict is based on the Dinosaur Brain's perception of the world. If companies are organized in a more cortical fashion, in which some real control is given to people lower down the corporate ladder, those employees will feel less inclined to accomplish aggressively what they can accomplish within the system. This in turn will save money and probably make companies better places to work.

You might want to try a thought experiment right now and think about how things would change at your company if the people below you rated you or the people in the next department rated your services. I can think of no better way to get the cortex operating.

Try this thought experiment. Imagine you're the head of a company or a large division. How and when would you know if:

One of your managers were a sadistic tyrant, a Captain Bligh, insulting and cruel to his staff, demanding more than is reasonable? In some companies the turnover of good people might be the first sign that the problem was serious. But the problem would show up sooner if his staff were rating his performance. Which of his staff would blow the whistle alone? If there were customer service ratings of his management style, you would be alerted that something untoward was going on.

How about sexual harassment? Would you have to wait until the papers were served to find out? This kind of activity builds up slowly over a long period. We generally punish people who tattle, so how would you know? When? How much would it cost you? How much is morale worth?

What if accounting and personnel were getting involved in a feud, and each was slowing down the other's requests and blocking progress at every turn? When would you find out it was a personality issue and not just day-to-day business? If each department's services were being rated by those who used them, there would be some low marks to investigate. Would you rely on the grapevine to give you this information? What system do you have now to report this kind of situation? Do you need to know?

What if your management team thought that you were at times difficult and unapproachable? What if they were afraid that you punish, rather than listen to, people who criticize you? What if they were just holding their tongues and seething? Would

you wait until the home office in New York called in an or-
ganization-development person to straighten things out, or would
you like to know sooner? Your customer service ratings would
have told you long before they heard about it in New York.

People gripe a lot to their peers, but productive gripes to superiors
need to be encouraged. The customer service model does that. Will
you buy it now?

17

Motivating Yourself and Your Employees

Business people often ask me, usually with exasperation, "How can I keep my employees motivated, and why do I have to worry about this? I pay them decently, so why should I have to spend time trying to get them to do what they should already be doing?"

Obviously, good wages are important, but they aren't the only reason employees keep coming to work every day. In addition to a paycheck, most people need to feel in control of and secure in their jobs, respected by their colleagues and supervisors, and hopeful about their professional futures: a part of the herd, as it were. People who don't feel this affiliation often leave. Good pay alone will not keep people in a place where they don't really feel a part of things. Employees are your company's biggest investment. No business can afford the regular loss of good people.

You can't assume that people will come to you already knowing what to do and how to do it, and brimming with the spirit to keep on doing it. A manager has to know how to motivate them and to consider motivational skills as an important part of any supervisory job.

Motivation involves encouraging your employees to use the creativity, enthusiasm, energy and loyalty from their Dinosaur Brains to contribute to their success and the company's. Following are some suggestions:

1. *Sell, don't tell.* Each of us has enough of the rebellious teenager inside to back up, slow down or mouth off if we're given too many direct orders at work. Being told what to do makes people angry. The most effective managers seldom issue commands. Instead, they see themselves as selling a course of action, and they use cajoling, persuading, bribing and rewarding far more often than a curt, "Do it."

Some dominant dinosaur types reading this will disagree and argue, "You have to be firm and in control." They'll often mention the military at this point. It's true that in the military in wartime, you can shoot people for not obeying orders. But this is seldom a cost-effective strategy in peacetime business.

If you tend to give direct orders, you can quickly maneuver yourself into having to punish or fire someone to maintain your authority. This can become destructive and expensive. Persuading people to do what they should is usually cheaper and more effective.

2. *See your actions from your employees' point of view.* Whatever motivates you may not be what motivates your employees. You might be a perfectionistic workaholic who couldn't live with yourself if you put in less than 150 percent effort and all your spare time at the office. There's a good chance that the people who work for you aren't similarly motivated.

If you expect them to be like you, you'll be trapped into disapproving of them and being angry with them for not being as motivated as you are. That disapproval will show, and it will erode your employees' trust in you. Credibility and trust are as important as paychecks.

3. *Listen, and let people know you are listening.* You don't have to do everything your employees want, but you do have to listen to them. The more you know about what they do and want, the more effective you'll be.

Try to schedule short, regular meetings, maybe 15 minutes once a week, or longer when necessary. Let them say what's on their minds, even if it means accepting criticism. Don't punish people for disagreeing. There's no surer way to stifle creativity.

If you set a meeting, don't cancel it. It's a slap in the face to the employees to be put aside for something else. You need to communicate that no one is more important than they are. At the meeting, *you* take the notes, and remember what was said the last time.

When employees complain to you, it's even more important that you listen carefully than that you take the action they request. They want you to know what it's like for them, and they'll be willing to work much harder if they think you care.

4. *Use goal-setting*. Research consistently shows that regular use of goal-setting improves performance more than any other technique. Define people's work in terms of goals and objectives. These need to be a basic part of each job, instead of something extra or tacked on. Every time you make a change in an employee's job without writing it down, you're throwing away a valuable management tool. The same mistake happens when you forget to do a written evaluation of a project or assignment.

To be effective as motivators, goals must be clear and reachable, and the employee has to know exactly what's required. If possible, state each goal in terms of what the employee must do, instead of what the outcome should be.

5. *Don't change dinosaurs midstream*. Your employees expect continuity from you. They expect you to remember what you told them to do yesterday and to be consistent in what you tell them today. If you aren't consistent, it feels as if nobody is really in control; they become distrustful and you lose credibility. Never mind that the CEO can't make up his mind and you keep getting contradictory messages. Your job is to insulate your people from inconsistencies from above, not to merely pass them on. If something you told your employees no longer applies, let them know it.

What we're really talking about here is memory. Unless yours is perfect, use a notebook.

6. *Follow through*. If you tell an employee that you're going to check on something for her, do it. Again, a notebook can be helpful. When you meet with employees, always carry your notebook. If you say you're going to do something, let them see that you're writing it down. Writing it in the book means that it's going to happen.

Review your notebook regularly and get back to people. Effective managers remember what they promise they're going to do, they do it and they let their employees know that it's done. If you don't intend to do something, don't say you will. Don't expect that people will forget a promise. Somebody will remember, and your credibility will go down.

7. *Build in a monitoring system.* Many managers use what I call a laissez-faire approach. As long as people seem to be doing what they're supposed to be doing, nobody pays much attention to them. When they obviously step out of line, they get zapped.

One of the many problems with this approach is that you don't know that something is wrong until there's a big problem. Then you have to check up and crack down, and the people involved will feel punished. Their Dinosaur Brains will activate and they'll start to fight back or run away.

It's much better to build monitoring systems into the daily course of the job so that you know what's going on. You can walk through your department every day, with your notebook, asking each person to give you a rundown on his or her projects or you can use elaborate management information systems. Whatever you do, do it consistently, not just when you think something is going wrong.

With a regular monitoring approach in place, your employees will expect you to check up on them, and they won't see it as criticism. Just be sure to monitor everyone, because people, true to their Dinosaur Brain instincts, will check on your checking.

8. *Avoid public ridicule.* Virtually all managers know not to chew out somebody when others are listening. But the most frequent form of public ridicule is a departmental memo that announces that the rules have been changed after someone has messed up. Everybody knows why the memo was sent and who made the mistake. Not only is the ridicule public, but it's in writing.

Also avoid telling people to come into your office only when you plan to criticize them. If that's your style, everyone will know what's going to happen.

9. *Delegate, don't dump.* Delegating is an important and essential management tool. The problem is that people often don't understand what it means. If you delegate unpleasant tasks that you don't want to do, that's called dumping. People will consider it, probably correctly, as an abuse of power. Delegation is giving something away that you wouldn't mind doing yourself, and giving enough authority to get it done.

10. *Give them something of their own.* Employees need as much authority over their own jobs as is possible and practical. If they have to check with you for every decision, they'll feel powerless and unnecessary. Give them the facts, and let them have a say in decisions that affect them. It's very demoralizing to feel that the chief lizards are settling their fate without even consulting them.

11. *Have a plan for their future.* People who can't move up, move out. If your corporate structure doesn't allow for promotions, you might think about changing it. Creating positions with better pay and more authority is a short-term cost that can yield long-term benefits if you're interested in keeping good employees.

Train people to fill better positions, and let them know you're grooming them. Even if they don't move up immediately, the possibility of promotion is an important motivator.

12. *Demonstrate commitment and respect.* If a person's job is secure, let him or her know it, especially if the company is going through a financial setback.

Be fair to everyone. Yelling at people, public criticism, negative gossip and personal feuds are self-indulgences few managers can afford. Set clear rules and stick to them. Your best employees will judge you by how you treat your worst.

13. *If you have a union, develop a working relationship.* Demonstrate your respect for union representatives by listening to them and acting on what they say. They will probably do the same for you.

14. *Encourage office friendship and socializing.* Obviously, this suggestion must be taken in moderation. Give people some time to talk and socialize at work. Employees stay on their jobs when they like the people they work with. Also make sure that people at different corporate levels have a chance to meet, not just at the office Christmas party, but often through the year. If employees have a chance to use the social nature of their Dinosaur Brains in a positive way at work, they'll return to their desks feeling energized and creative as their cortex takes over.

15. *Offer new training and challenges.* If people feel they can grow in their jobs, they're more likely to stay with them.

16. *Use rewards and incentives.* If you're thinking, "I do use rewards, I give them a paycheck," then this advice is aimed directly at you. You have some serious reconsidering to do. What you say to people right after they do something well is much more important than a paycheck later.

If you want to get better at management styles that generate feelings of loyalty and affiliation, learn to manage like a woman. Studies are showing that, in general, women are better than men at using positive and affiliative approaches.

People respond to praise, and if you don't use it, you're trying to do your job with outdated equipment. The recommended ratio of praise to punishment at work is four to one. Unfortunately, most managers give out criticism four times as often as compliments. You can catch more dinosaurs with honey.

18

Stress Is Not the Enemy

Some people automatically consider job stress dangerous and bad, which is not necessarily true. In moderate levels, stress can be beneficial psychologically and physically. Like exercise.

Stress is what's happening out there in the world. It can be deadlines, phones ringing, too many job demands, too many meetings, or the ever-present difficulties of dealing with other people. We can't really define stress in absolute terms. Instead, it has to be defined by its effects on people.

Some people see a threat and act on it; others react. It is their internal response that causes the problem. In Chapter 4, we saw that the inappropriate triggering of the "fight, flight or fright" response creates potentially harmful changes, such as increased heart and breathing rates, overworked adrenal glands, tense muscles, and so forth. This response often leaves people physiologically in the state of going uphill in high gear, which causes a great deal of stress on the body and the psyche.

The level of arousal can be measured, and this level determines how stressful a particular situation is to a person. It's important to measure these responses, because it's often possible for people to deny that stress has any effect on them. Your family doctor or mental health practitioner can give you information about how to measure your level of arousal. A simple method is to be aware of an accelerated heartbeat and count your pulse rate. Muscle tension, especially in the neck and shoulders and around the jaws, is another sign of hyperarousal. High blood pressure can be another indication.

Over time, it's possible to learn to lower your response to stress. This process is known as coping. People use all sorts of coping strategies, some of which are healthy and make them stronger, but others undermine their ability to deal with stress.

Stress-Hardiness

Most of you have seen that stress test on which you assign points to life changes, and if you get too many points, you're supposed to get sick or have a nervous breakdown within a year.

Recently there was a study of executives who scored very high on the life-change scale but did not get sick. These managers were called *stress hardy*. They seemed to flourish in situations that would severely damage other people. How did they do it? Their most effective coping strategy was a set of beliefs about life and the job. Central were beliefs about:

Control. These executives believed that what they did made a difference in the overall scheme of things and never considered that their problems were someone else's fault.

Commitment. The hardy managers felt that they were where they should be. They had not necessarily achieved all the success that they wanted, but they felt that they were in the right line of work and the right relationships and had the right hobbies. This feeling resulted less from believing they had made lucky choices than from their tendency to really get behind their decisions once they were made.

Challenge. The hardy executives regarded setbacks as problems to be solved, rather than as catastrophes. They were likely to respond to a loss in one area of their lives by taking on a challenge in another area, such as coping with divorce by learning a foreign language. These people had the capacity to soothe themselves through self-improvement.

You can learn to be hardier by acting as if you see life in the way that these executives did. Acting as if you're in control is just as good as being in control.

The bad news is that studies also show that people who most need stress-hardiness tend to prevent themselves from making the changes that would help them. They read a chapter like this and respond by thinking, "I'll do it tomorrow," or "I already know all that, but it doesn't really apply in my case," or "I don't have time." All of these excuses come straight from the part of the Dinosaur Brain that tries to protect you from new ideas.

Some coping strategies are especially unhealthy because they tend to increase your arousal over the long run. Drugs and alcohol immediately come to mind. These strategies also include getting angry; looking at a problem to decide whose fault it is; organizing your job so that it's never finished (the workaholic syndrome); and avoiding the difficult parts of your job by forgetting or being too busy to deal with them.

Coping Techniques

How should you deal with stress? All of the stress hardy attitudes discussed here aren't necessarily the beliefs people were born with. You can learn them and practice them daily. Studies show that people who adopt these attitudes and work with them tend to be much more resistant to stresses of all kinds.

1. *Maintain a positive attitude.* How you see the situations of your life determines whether those events are stressful and how much negative arousal you're going to experience. It's what you tell yourself about the world—not the world itself—that causes problems.

Survivors and successful people tend to share the attitude, however erroneous, that they have some control over what happens to them.

I don't really have to tell you this, since you bought this book and are reading it. You obviously feel that you can do something to make things better for yourself.

2. *Stick with a decision.* Decide that quitting is not an option. When you've made your choice, accept it happily; the best decisions are created after they're made.

3. *Think of setbacks as challenges instead of disasters.* Let your cortex control, even if you're upset. Don't tap into the "If It Hurts, Hiss!" section of your Dinosaur Brain. (Chapter 8 discussed this expression of Lizard Logic.)

Most conventional sources on stress advise you to cut down on the number of challenges you face, but it seems that really hardy people have developed ways to use new situations to respond to losses in other areas of their lives and to improve themselves at the same time.

4. *Exercise, eat a balanced diet, take care of yourself.* Obviously, it's important in dealing with stress to do all the things that the stress-management books tell you to do. Take care of your body, and it will take care of you.

5. *Always take the time to have fun.* Laughter and humor can take you out of Dinosaur Brain thinking, because the Dinosaur Brain has no sense of humor. It doesn't have the equipment to see anything as funny. The lizard world is deadly serious. Whenever you're laughing, your body is adjusting itself and your stress level is going down.

6. *Learn a technique to lower your physiological arousal on demand.* Know what relaxing is and how to do it. The technique I use most often involves exploiting a defect in the central nervous system— your brain cannot tell reality from fantasy. Basically, when you think of a situation in which you're relaxed and calm, your brain can fool your body into believing that relaxation is the appropriate response. Want to try it?

This technique has many names—imagery, self-hypnosis, relaxation training. Call it what you like. Here's how to do it:

Relaxation Technique

Make some time and space for yourself.
When you begin, don't do it where there is a lot of noise. Sit
in a comfortable chair.
Close your eyes,
take a deep breath.
Imagine the most pleasant, relaxing place you can picture.
A beach, perhaps.
Try to bring to mind the scene as vividly as possible,
using all your senses.
You might close your eyes and see the brilliant blue of the sky
and the slow, stately shapes of clouds moving across the sky.
Look out in the distance and see waves breaking on the shore;
see the shimmer of heat rising from the sand.
With the ears of your mind, hear the sea sounds.
With every wave you imagine, you might pretend that the water is
washing away tension.
You're becoming more and more relaxed.
Let your tensions float out to sea.
Feel the waves of relaxation breaking inside your body,
washing your tension away.
Can you smell the sea salt,
the faint fishy smell of the beach,
or the warm cool scent of the suntan cream?
The more you can remember and imagine,
the more vivid your fantasy will become.
People can feel in their mind as well.
Imagine what it feels like to lie on the sand
and feel the warm sun on your skin,
a cool breeze on your face as you lie on the quiet beach.
As you relax, you may notice that your body feels heavier and heavier
as more of your weight is transferred to the chair in which
you're sitting.
Maybe you've noticed this feeling when you lie down at night
after a hard day, and your body seems
to sink deeper and deeper into the bed.
Just for practice, make your body as heavy as possible now.
Let it sink into your chair as you read this page.
You may notice that you're feeling more relaxed, more calm.

Search for any areas of tension in your body and see how
pleasantly heavy you can make them.
It might be fun to imagine yourself sinking into a cloud, or
the softest feather bed in the world.
Just allow yourself to go as deeply into the relaxation as you want to.
You can stay here for as long as you wish.

When you're ready, you can return to your normal state of alertness, feeling relaxed and refreshed, and realizing that you have gained some control over your physiological responses just by using your imagination.

19

Is Your Mind Out of Shape?

Even though the brain isn't a muscle, it sometimes works like one. If you continue to think in the same ways, day after day and year after year, your mind gets sluggish. An out-of-shape mind can still do plenty of work but not as efficiently. You lose creativity, flexibility and the ability to handle change.

The Dinosaur Brain leads us to think according to a few time-honored patterns that are considered universal truth rather than opinions. Minds that know rather than think run to fat very quickly.

What are the signs of mental flab? You won't see a spare tire around your head, so here's what to look for:

Irritation at Changes in Routine. People whose thinking has gotten out of shape automatically distrust the unfamiliar or different. When someone suggests a new idea, their immediate reactions tend to be negative. They cover up their fear by marshalling facts to prove that the suggested change would do no good. "We tried that in 1968 and it didn't work."

People with mental sluggishness also tend to see new developments in their field as simply reworks of old concepts. They like to use the word "fad" to describe almost anything other than the tried and true.

Limited Areas of Interest and Concern. Out-of-shape minds start seeing the world from their own limited point of view. ("Will the drought in Africa be good or bad for small-appliance sales?") They tend to act bored or irritated when someone brings up other subjects in conversation that don't center on their own small universe.

Reuse of Old Material. People whose minds are going to seed tend gleefully to repeat the same comments and anecdotes over and over:

"Well, it just goes to show you. . . ."

"You get what you pay for."

"The problem with business today is the erosion of the work ethic."

"It's those blankety-blank Republicans."

"It's those blankety-blank Democrats."

"Workers in my day had more. . . ."

What happens in the world no longer shapes or changes their viewpoints. Instead, they tend to distort whatever is going on to fit the two or three guiding principles that control their thinking. ("The erosion of the work ethic" is a favorite.)

Flat Emotions. When a mind is out of shape, there is no excitement. Excitement comes from, among other sources, taking risks, and that's what sedentary minds do least well. Narrowing their focus prevents people from having to deal with situations that are unfamiliar. They stop learning anything.

People with mental flab don't experience much anxiety; instead they feel a kind of low-level boredom. There is real danger that this boredom can be covered with alcohol or drugs. Usually this does not mean heavy drinking, but a drinking pattern that, like everything else they do, is persistent, orderly and predictable. In the long run, it is just as destructive as any other form of alcohol abuse.

Seeing People and Things as Good or Bad, Right or Wrong. One of the hallmarks of a mind that is not working up to capacity is the assumption that things fall into only two possible categories. Lapsing into the Dinosaur Brain's "Just like me, good; not like me, bad" program, rather than puzzling out complicated issues of morality, is a sign of an out-of-shape mind. ("There are two ways to do things: a right way and a wrong way." Typically, the wrong category is about five times the size of the right.)

Decreased Ability to Concentrate. To concentrate and think clearly, a mind has to be in top working order. People whose minds have gotten flabby tend to have short attention spans and difficulty in concentrating. Often they will cover this by saying they are too busy and have too many things to think about. In reality, the ability to focus just isn't there any more.

If your mind is out of shape, try Bernstein's Mental Aerobics.

Learn Something New on a Regular Basis. Once a month or so, read a book by someone with different political views from your own. Men, read a book on feminism. Women, read Hemingway. At least read something outside your area of interest. Poetry is a good choice because it seems to be outside everyone's area of interest. Even at its worst, poetry is the human endeavor that is farthest from Dinosaur Brain thinking.

Take a class. Put yourself on the line by trying something new to you. Take a chance. Bring up new subjects in conversation. Risk not being the authority.

Break Routines. Spend time with different people. Watch different television shows, or no TV at all for awhile. Resist using the same old phrases. Take a new route to work.

Listen for a Change. Mentally flabby dinosaurs never listen. They know what other people are going to say and they know what's true. To them listening is a waste of time. There's no point listening when you know everything already.

Listening can also be a new and enlightening experience, especially when people are talking about you. You might ask your spouse or friends about your thinking patterns and whether you seem to be in a rut. Maybe other people you know are feeling the same type of sluggishness, and you could work on this mental aerobics program together.

Make a pact to discuss new topics at your next get-together. No talking allowed about jobs, kids or sports.

Take a Stand and Defend It. Learn enough about something that interests you in the news, your community or office to develop an opinion about it. Discuss your point of view with someone who doesn't agree; care enough to defend it intelligently. You'll stretch your mind and gain self-confidence (as well as a new conversational topic for your mental-aerobics group.)

Teach Something. There is nothing like teaching to make you really think about an area. Lizard Logic falls apart when you think of spouting it in front of a roomful of inquiring minds.

Try Some Physical Exercise—It Couldn't Hurt. Studies show that regular exercise not only improves the body but the thinking process as well.

When people start this kind of mental exercise regimen, they often make all sorts of plans to do different things, but when the time comes to do them, they slip back into their old routines. One of the ways around this tendency is to schedule something new every week in your appointment book. We all do what our appointment books say.

Go for it!

20

Long-Term Planning

Long-term planning is an alien concept to the Dinosaur Brain, which is always more concerned with the next meal or the next threat (such as the bottom line for the coming fiscal quarter). But ignoring long-term planning at work is choosing the road to extinction.

Everyone deplores crisis management, but everyone does it, not because there are so many crises, but because it's more fun. We're also programmed to do it that way. To change the pattern from professional near-sightedness to long-term planning, some excitement must be injected into a dreary cortical task.

Nobody really sees into the future. The two functions of long-term planning are to set some measurable goals so you know where you're heading and to develop a flexible organization that can respond coherently and cooperatively to crisis or change.

Self-Management

The most common complaint of businesspeople is that they have no time. I've seen lots of time-management courses and I've realized that even the title is misleading, because you really can't manage time. No matter what you do, there will always be 24 hours in the day. What you can do is manage yourself and decide how you're going to use the 24 hours. So time-management is really self-management.

A company that operates with a "no time for it" mentality is blocked by one or more of these problems:

1. There's no top management support for planning. The company makes no effort to form a working team to deal with crises. Instead, people are pulled together catch-as-catch-can when a crisis occurs. Long-term planning is usually surprisingly short-range and is often done by a few people who are at the top.

2. Planning is usually reserved for a retreat setting. People get together once every quarter (or even less frequently) at the coast or in the mountains and the session ends up as recreation or as an airing of personality problems.

3. Any goals for the long term, say five or ten years, are usually not concrete. For example, often companies don't set a maximum-profits goal, which can cause problems in a couple of ways. First, if the company has a really good year financially, this changes the expectations of its investors and employees so that, in the next year when performance is more typical, people think the company is losing ground, rather than having gained it in the long run. Second, a business must be able to say how much profit is enough so that it can start using the money elsewhere.

4. Planning is often one-dimensional. It's too easy to focus on one part of the corporate picture at the expense of others, depending on which department or manager is dominant. Many companies, for example, are finance-driven. Next quarter's bottom line may prevent action that might lead to improved profits ten years down the line.

Also in planning, companies tend to focus on their own actions and sometimes ignore the fact that they're part of an international economy that fluctuates.

5. Most planning is done with no idea of company history. George Santayana said, "Those who cannot remember the past are condemned to repeat it." By looking at a company's history, you can get an idea of its past priorities and decide whether to stick with them.

History will often tell you what will happen if you plan inadequately or not at all. You can learn more from past mistakes in your own or other companies than from past successes. Many businesses tend to repeat a successful formula until it becomes unsuccessful. How many times, for instance, can the Big Three make the same car?

Corporate histories are becoming best-sellers, along with the memoirs of great managers (or people who consider themselves great managers). As companies become more aware of corporate culture, I predict that more and more businesses will create the position of corporate historian—the in-house professional cortex.

6. Most of all, planning is dull. The Dinosaur Brain usually gets in the way of planning, but it can also offer a few ideas to make planning easier.

What Usually Happens in Planning Sessions

First, if you call a meeting for long-term planning, a lot of people tend to beg off immediately, saying they're too busy and they don't have time to plan any farther ahead than tomorrow at two o'clock. Many people dismiss long-term planning as a pastime of people with nothing better to do.

Second, other people will attend the meeting, knowing that their input isn't really wanted and they're just there to listen to the bosses predict the future. Still others, who weren't invited, tend to resent planning sessions because they only hear about them later, in the form of a list of how things are going to be in the company from now on. They feel they have no input.

Third, at the meeting, a bunch of people sit around spinning yarns about what they think will happen. They've read somebody's gloom-and-doom predictions and bring them up. Planning, if it's done at all, will be very superficial. Often people will accept the plan presented by the person with the most dominant or verbal personality. Everybody else sits and listens.

This is no fun at all. Here are suggestions for making your planning sessions effective:

1. *Get support from the top.* If you don't have the CEO or chairman behind you, you're not going to be able to make a long-term plan for the whole company. If top management support is not forthcoming, you might limit your planning to the largest division whose manager agrees to participate. A two-person commitment to planning will not do, unless those two people have authority over everybody else at the meeting.

2. *Know your goal.* Put together a flexible team that works well together under pressure. This goal is often better than having a set plan because set plans can never cover all contingencies.

3. *Make planning a regular part of the job.* Get together for planning sessions, or use some other methods, on a regular basis. Don't wait for stability—in business, you're always up to your rear end in lizards. The important thing is what you do when you're up to your rear end in lizards. It doesn't take much creativity just to cut back on everything so the quarter doesn't look disastrous.

4. *Continue having your retreats,* but use them for dealing with personality and communication problems. It's very good to have a structure to deal with these issues because they will always come up.

5. *Make the planning exciting,* and structure it so that people will deal with the unexpected in unexpected ways. Most managers see an assignment to come up with a five-year plan for their department as dull beyond belief; it's not their style of working. When planning is made to seem more like a combat drill in a peacetime army, dinosaurs can really sink their teeth into it.

6. *Make the planning count for something.* People who come up with good ideas and accurate plans should get rewards and recognition, just as the ones do who save the bacon in emergencies.

7. *Involve as many people as possible.* Make planning a regular part of everybody's work week. Structuring it like a game or competition can often draw participation. Let everybody know what's going on and that you want their ideas. The Dinosaur Brain works best in a crowd.

8. *Keep a present orientation.* Just talking about the future in the present tense will make it more interesting and more real. Remember that the Dinosaur Brain has no imagination.

9. *Eat an elephant one bite at a time.* Coming up with a whole plan is a horrendous task. Restrict planning to short sessions dealing with one issue at a time.

10. *Don't forget to write down and condense the results.*

Here are a couple of planning games to give you ideas for developing long-term strategy:

The Midnight Meeting. In brushfire management, the usual vehicle is the midnight meeting, in which people are told to drop everything and be there to save the company. This is obnoxious to most people and gets in the way of doing their regular jobs. But it *is* exciting. You can schedule meetings like this and bring up a planning issue as if it were a crisis happening right now. You can present it as a hypothetical crisis.

You could begin, for example, by saying, "Ladies and gentlemen, the prime rate goes up to 20 percent. What will be the effect on your department?" The idea is to get people into the habit of responding to crises and to work out a style of doing so. Very quickly you'll be able to see some of the hitches, who participates and who doesn't, who tends to run the show and whose ideas tend to be most accurate.

The Futurist Book. Have everybody on the management team read the same futurist book, then come in and discuss how the company can meet the challenges the author has outlined. As the team gets better at this, you can deal with more long-term and far-reaching problems.

If you simply wait for a crisis, you're apt to have a lot more Dinosaur Brain decisions. If you practice coping with crises in advance, people will have some experience in moderating their Dinosaur Brain reactions with their cortical thinking.

The Competitive Edge. The Dinosaur Brain really enjoys competition. You can take advantage of this raw enthusiasm by dividing your planning meeting into teams and having them compete for the best plan. While you're at it, you can have one group plan for your competition. It's more interesting when you have real bad guys to fight than when you merely talk about what they might do.

Planning can be made more exciting by involving the Dinosaur Brain. To do that, make your planning sessions short, competitive and immediate. They must seem less like planning and more like "really doing."

The Dinosaur Brain can't plan by itself, but without its help, the cortex never gets started. An idle Dinosaur Brain will always find something more interesting to do than sit around and play cortical games.

21

Making Waves

Right now, list your top three professional achievements.

As soon as you've finished that, list your top three skills.

If you're like most people, your heartbeat just speeded up, your breathing grew short and shallow, and maybe your mind started to go blank. In short, the Triple F Response. Why did that happen? Your reaction would have been even worse if I had asked you to imagine that you were reciting your achievements list in front of a group of co-workers or, heaven forbid, your boss. Yet you wouldn't have panicked if I'd asked you to name the last five presidents of the United States.

Why is saying good things about yourself such a big deal? The vague discomfort you feel about it and your perception of it as a dangerous act come from your Dinosaur Brain.

In Chapter 5, we focused mostly on the highly aggressive types vying constantly to get ahead a little quicker. Most of us hold back in that respect, trying to avoid the pace of the fast lane. We prefer to remain with the herd, moving along at our own pace. Our Dinosaur Brain warns us that self-promotion is an aggressive act, a bid to upset the system and push us out to that dangerous fast lane.

The negative feelings about making waves are particularly common in professionals in private practice. Many of us think that selling ourselves is beneath us, that all we have to do is be good at what we are trained to do and the world will beat a path to our door. But who's going to know how good you are if nobody has ever heard of you? That shingle on the front is awfully small.

The distaste that many professionals feel for self-promotion comes from the Dinosaur Brain. Preserving the hierarchy is important to practitioners in particular. Without the hierarchy that gives people with certain degrees extra status, our training would mean nothing. I'm not saying that professionals should advertise as some recently have begun to do, but we should realize that we have some control over what our image will be. In most urban areas, competition in the professions is increasing. Although the ideas discussed in this chapter are mostly stated in a corporate context, they apply to professionals in private practice as well.

So far we've talked about how the Dinosaur Brain activates responses, but it also tends to tone down certain responses. One of the aspects of our dominance pattern is to be good members of the hierarchy, to trust it and not make waves. We come programmed with resistance to change and to advancing ourselves over others.

From childhood we are told not to be conceited. As adults we hear negative names for corporate self-promotion: people call it brownnosing, playing politics, apple-polishing, all said in a tone of voice that makes it sound truly awful. Indeed, if you think of the olfactory connotations of brownnosing, you'll understand.

After our teenage rebellions, most of us settle in as responsible members of the company hierarchy, and we look disdainfully on anyone who does something to rock the boat. Yet we hope for promotions and believe that, if we do a good job, we'll be rewarded.

We need to check out that belief. Virtually all promotions are self-promotions. The day you stop promoting yourself is the day you stop advancing. Your Dinosaur Brain will tell you that merely doing a good job is enough, and if this were the ideal world, perhaps it would be.

If we want to be leaders and to move up, we have to *display* leadership behaviors, not just carry them out quietly. We must make certain that the people who make decisions about our futures see us behaving as leaders.

Chapter 28 discusses how to fit well into the hierarchy and make the dinosaurs think you're worthy of being one of them. This chapter deals with getting that promotion by promoting yourself.

Let's take another look at the belief that if you do a good job, you'll be rewarded. First, how do you know you're doing a good job? List your answers here:

1. _____

2. _____

3. _____

4. _____

That might have been a little easier than your first assignment at the beginning of this chapter, but it's still hard. Usually you're talking about internal feelings, or the fact that you got other promotions, or that nobody has told you you're doing a bad job. Doing this exercise might help you see that you're doing a good job because of certain things that you are, certain skills you have and certain actions you take. You might keep working at this list until you have some clear ideas about what you have done and what your skills are.

Next ask yourself, Who needs to know? If you're going to get a promotion, who needs to be aware that you're good at what you do, and how will this person be able to find out? Do you think he or she reads your personnel files or asks supervisors for lists of people who are worthy of promotion? It would be nice if this happened (and some people indeed do it), but mostly you can't assume that the people above you have any more orderly ways of getting their information than you do.

Let's talk about self-promotion. What do the people above you need in their employees? Do you have it? How can you let them know you have it? If you're a professional and aren't as booked up or as fast-track as you'd like to be, maybe you can think about a couple of promotional concepts, short of taking out a full-page ad in the Yellow Pages or newspaper.

Here are some ideas for practicing self-promotion.

1. Have a clear concept of what the product—you—is and what it can do. Spend some time thinking about your top skills and accomplishments. This can be difficult; you can carry a mental image of yourself as a good and qualified person, but it's hard to get down to specifics. It's harder still to actually say the words, "I'm better than most people at. . . ." Your Dinosaur Brain keeps screaming, "Watch out! If you raise yourself up, somebody will knock you down." The only hubris most of us allow ourselves is being holier than thou.

Often it's helpful to begin by talking about yourself in the third person. It's a lot easier to compliment other people than to compliment ourselves. When we start praising ourselves, our Dinosaur Brains flash warning signals. We have to feel very sure indeed before we say anything good about ourselves.

2. Once you come up with a list of your good points, skills and achievements, practice saying them: "I am a good manager," or "I know more about computer simulation than anybody else in this company," or "I'm flexible; I'm good at dealing coolly with crises" or whatever is true about you.

Now think about your list and how it fits in with what your company needs, what it's looking for in new leaders, what its challenges will be and what talent it will require. Keep this short, one or two items. We'll call this area of overlap your persona or mask. This is the product you're going to sell; this is what you need to advertise and promote.

3. To sell yourself, you'll need a general idea of the direction you want to go. The books on success that tell you to plot your career course for five years make the situation too simple. It's very difficult to know where you'll be in five years, but you do have a general idea of whether you want to stay with the company or gain experiences that will send you outside. You also have a sense of what kind of responsibilities you'd like to have.

4. Begin your advertising with name association. Assume that when people think of you, they will store your name, a mental picture of you, a few words they associate with you and a few stories about your behavior. From this they will make all the decisions that they have to make about you.

Name association is a good start for promoting yourself because you can do it in a self-deprecating way. Decide what you want people to remember when they think of you. Then say things about yourself that create those images.

You can say,

> "I'm just an old war-horse. I've been around here forever"
>
> or
>
> "Back in 1967, when I started managing in this division. . . ."
>
> or
>
> "I can look at this issue from several different perspectives. I started out in engineering, then went through marketing, and now I'm in product development. I can tell you, they look at the world differently in all those places."

All of these are ways of linking your name to experience.

If flexibility is your forte, you might talk about all the different things you've done and describe yourself as a jack-of-all-trades and master of none, which at times can be quite a positive quality.

A young dinosaur, eager for promotion, might use a variation of one of these self-descriptions:

> "Me, I eat, sleep and dream software."
>
> "In a way, my job is my hobby. I'm always trying to design the better mousetrap."
>
> "I'm a people person. My strong point is seeing everybody else's strong points."

5. Tell stories, the more vivid the better. Instead of talking about your management philosophy, tell people, "Here's what happened in my department. . . . This is what I said to Bill . . . and this is the effect it had. . . ." People will forget the concept, but they'll remember the story.

6. Never miss a chance to do a presentation to management— not for what you say, but for the effect you have on the audience. When you're standing in front of a group of people, this is just about the only chance you'll have to be a leader of leaders.

Your Dinosaur Brain will tell you to stick to facts, be cautious, cover your tail, but when you're in front of people is the time to demonstrate your own specific skills and ways of thinking.

One way to do this is to begin by making the presentation that everybody expects to hear. Then, instead of making the expected conclusion, throw in some sort of surprise and show them how the line of reasoning might not be what they thought it was. This will get their attention, then you can tell stories. Finally, demonstrate that you've done your homework by including piles and piles of handouts of facts and figures in the presentation. People will remember that you had a quantity of information, but they will seldom analyze it.

7. Don't ever wait for a job to open up and then compete for it. Always be on the lookout for new career opportunities that are cropping up. Propose a new position to those in power along with the idea that you are the person to do it. Don't be someone who waits until the opening goes up on the bulletin board. The best job for you is probably the one you invent.

8. Once you've done all of these other things, say "No" to your Dinosaur Brain once more and actually ask for the money. All of us are in marketing and sales in one way or another. What separates the good sales reps from the poor ones is that the good salespeople know how to close the sale. Anybody can talk about how great the product is; the good sales rep always asks for the money or the signature on the dotted line.

Your Dinosaur Brain will tell you, "Wait! It's too soon! You could get punished! You might look silly!" but once you've presented your case, the next step is to say, "I want to do it. When do I start?" You'll never get a job you don't ask for.

22

It's Lonely at the Top

It's surprising how often people who are successful in their jobs have so few friends. Even more surprising is how many people have no friends and don't even realize it. I'm not talking about eccentric geniuses or reclusive workaholics. The people to whom I'm referring are most often (but not always) men in middle and upper management.

To subordinates, these executives seem like king lizards, basking in the privileges of territory, dominance and power. There they go, part of the Old Boys' network, sauntering off with the CEO to an expense-account lunch or a weekend on the company yacht.

Many of these men are actually more like solitary dinosaurs, alone on their hilltops, eyeing each other from across the valley and keeping wary watch over their herds. They are bright, competent and still on their way up. They know instinctively that, if you're a manager, you can be friendly with the people you work with, but you can't really be friends. There are too many things you just wouldn't or shouldn't confide to your colleagues or subordinates.

Brad is a middle manager in a lizard-infested corporation. His voice sounds wistful when he talks about his lack of friends. "No, I don't have a circle of good buddies," he says. "I didn't get where I am by being Mr. Nice Guy. I work fourteen-hour days and a lot of Saturdays. When I go home, I crash. I don't feel comfortable with the social chitchat at the parties my wife and I are invited to. They're always her friends who invite us, and I don't really have anything in common with the other husbands. What do they know, or care, about what it's like to sit through a takeover with your job on the line? I guess making new friends just isn't a high priority. I'm too damn busy."

Many executives may be very good at professional relationships—conversing for a purpose—but they aren't comfortable with real socializing, which they consider merely making idle chitchat. They're too busy and too exhausted to try to meet new people, as some self-help books advise. The result is that they don't have many friendships to count on when they need emotional support.

Women managers face special problems with loneliness. If they've reached an executive position, there almost certainly aren't many other women at their level within the company. Making friends with male colleagues can be difficult because the Old Boys' network still doesn't include Old Girls. They know from the management books that it's a mistake to pal around with the secretaries.

Female managers can find themselves out of touch with women whose jobs aren't as competitive as their own. If they are working mothers, they don't feel they have enough time in their hectic schedules for a "luxury" like maintaining close friendships.

Sometimes managers of both sexes are too busy to notice that they're lonely. More often, they don't recognize the real cause of the discomfort they feel. They are letting their Dinosaur Brains set the rules: a rigid sense of morality ("Work is more important and less ambiguous than friendships"); dominance ("Don't socialize with underlings") and territoriality ("My job is my place").

They can experience boredom and apathy, the sense that things just aren't fun any more. Usually these feelings are especially strong away from work, although later the lack of interest creeps into the office too. Nothing gets the juices flowing.

Boredom can lead to abuse of power. The chief dinosaur can do anything he wants and sometimes resorts to complicated head-games with subordinates to alleviate the boredom. Meddling in the lives of mortals has been the sport of gods since Zeus began dating human girls.

Affairs can provide the semblance of intimacy. People without friends can easily fall into affairs as a substitute for friendships. These relationships tend to be short-term, however, and seem to cause more problems than they solve by further isolating the people involved. (See Chapter 25 for a complete discussion of why people get involved in office romances.)

Marital and family problems abound when you become so used to paying attention to other things that you forget how to get along with people day-to-day. You can become irritable when people want something from you, when you have so much important work to do.

Alcohol abuse can be another sign of emotional isolation. It becomes a pattern to go home from work and drink, perhaps not heavily, but steadily and alone, until sleep comes. The lonely cycle begins again the next morning.

Emotionally isolated executives often have the feeling that there is no one they can really talk to, no one who really understands them. It doesn't occur to them that, to be understood, you have to explain yourself.

Often they hide their loneliness from themselves by being overly dependent on one person, such as a spouse or subordinate. This kind of over-dependence can lead to petty tyranny, disappointment at the tiniest slight, and demands that the other person be there at all times and in all ways. It's easy to imagine what these demands can do to a marriage or a working relationship.

How to Tell if You Don't Have Enough Friends

Who would you talk to if you had doubts about yourself, failed at a project at work or made a big mistake? Who would be there to listen if you had a problem you needed to talk about?

If you can't think of three people, you probably don't have enough real friends.

Many self-help books say, if you don't have enough friends, just go out and make some. For a man or woman who works killer hours in a high-pressure job, this is easier said than done. Making friends requires an investment of time, effort and energy, not to mention the risk of rejection.

Kate has her own business, two school-age children and a husband who also works long hours. She remembers the days, pre-kids and pre-business, when she and her women friends got together for lunches, hour-long phone calls, Saturday shopping sprees and monthly nights out. She doesn't remember what they talked about, but she remembers the laughter and the closeness, the feeling that when things just got to be too much, she wouldn't have to cope alone.

Now that her children are so active and her career has taken off, it just seems like too much of an effort to get together with her friends. When Kate leaves her office, she goes home to do her family's cooking, laundry, cleaning and shopping. On weekends there are the kids' activities, errands to run, elderly parents to visit or call, and maybe dinner out and a movie with her husband. Yet there are times when she feels an ache inside, missing the friends she used to confide in. When Kate looks at the calendar, she thinks it must be too late to find those women again.

It may not be too late at all. Reconnecting with old friends and former colleagues—the people you cared about and spent time with when you and the world were both a bit younger—may be a realistic and valuable choice.

Instead of long phone calls several times a week, this time around the friendship might thrive on breakfast or lunch once a month, notes or postcards that say, "I'm thinking of you" even when there's no time to get together and a real heart-to-heart a few times a year, when one of you needs it most.

Sometimes you have to go back farther than a few years. For many of us, our student days were the last time we were a part of a large peer group with time for socializing. I wonder what your college roommates are doing now. Go ahead, reach out and touch someone. You may be surprised at how long an early friendship can last.

Have you made friends with your parents yet? If that possibility exists for you, closeness across family generations can be an important source of emotional support.

"But I'm an adult," you say, "and even if my parents would be willing to treat me like one, there's no way they would be able to follow every twist and turn of the merger details, or even begin to understand who I really am now." Maybe so, but they might surprise you with how well they can still keep up with you. Don't forget, they knew you when.

How to Reconnect

If you've decided to make time for friends again, here are a few ideas to get you started:

1. Realize that you have to make an effort in the beginning to make yourself available.

Consider getting to know some of the people outside of work who share a few of your interests. Some great friendships have begun from conversations between neighbors over the lawn mower on a Saturday afternoon. Maybe you've already volunteered to help with your child's Little League team or joined the Parents' Club at church. You might be taking tennis or racquetball lessons on the weekend. Maybe you're involved in a community group to save your neighborhood school or collect food for hungry families.

Any of these can be a natural setting for friendships. You wouldn't be out there at the Little League field, clutching a wad of business cards, networking feverishly. You'd be sitting in the bleachers with the other moms and dads, cheering for each other's kids and chatting between innings. No big deal. It could be the perfect place to discover another closet Chicago Cubs' fan or a kindred soul who confesses that he, like you, would really rather be home playing chess.

2. Don't expect other people to call you. Make the first move yourself. Invite someone to lunch or to dinner. Schedule a specific time, instead of offering a vague invitation like "Let's get together sometime." For the lonely dinosaur, sometime never comes.

Think of the possibilities for friendship during the time you have available: a lunch hour or coffee break, a quick phone call from the office or after the kids are in bed, a special dinner with your spouse at a nice restaurant on a weekend night.

These days everybody's busy, and a once-a-year renewal of a bygone friendship can be a welcome gift for both of you instead of a source of guilt because you don't see each other more often. You might want to establish a tradition with an old friend: meeting for a long lunch during the Christmas season, an annual reunion in your home town, a family picnic.

3. Signal to other people that you want to spend time with them. Don't cancel appointments or find excuses to avoid socializing. If you've set a lunch date with someone, don't decide that you're just too busy to go out that day.

4. Make friendship an active priority. Realize that you need other people in your life. Remember that, as you get older, it's more difficult to make friends, but the friends you make are much more important.

Think the next time you find yourself sharing a joke with a neighbor whose sense of humor is as off the wall as yours, or have coffee with a well-read colleague whose desk is just as littered with "To do" lists as yours. Before you just wave goodbye and hurry back to the weeds, or scuttle back to your corporate cave, remember the last line from *Casablanca*. For you, too, this could be the start of a beautiful friendship.

23

The Captain Kirk Management Style

In an episode of "Star Trek" (maybe you remember it), the senior officers of the Enterprise were contaminated by low-level radiation from a comet, which caused them to age rapidly and prematurely. Forty-five minutes into the program, Kirk, Spock, Bones and Scotty had aged to the point that they could no longer carry out their duties. They were confined to the sick bay while the crew feverishly sought an antidote.

The situation was pretty bleak, and grew worse. While upper management was thus incapacitated, the Romulans attacked.

Remember the scene on the bridge? Sulu, Uhura and the other remaining officers nervously looking at each other while the force field screens were taking a pounding. Nobody knew quite what to do. Then, just in the nick of time, an antidote—adrenaline—was found in the sick bay, and the senior officers were back in action.

Maybe you remember the feeling of relief as the door to the bridge swished open, and there was Captain Kirk, young again and ready to take charge. I cheered. Within minutes, the Romulans were no longer a problem. No question about it: James T. Kirk knew how to handle a Romulan attack. What a manager! Or was he?

Years later, when I became a business consultant, I remembered this "Star Trek" episode and began to have nagging doubts about Captain Kirk's management style. Why didn't other officers know what to do during the Romulan attack? It seems that Enterprise, Inc. had a few problems developing the skills and responsibilities of middle management.

In our culture there is some confusion between management and heroics. The distinction is actually quite simple: The hero handles everything single-handedly; the manager delegates. If a manager is indispensable, is he or she really managing?

The Dinosaur Brain says that the person at the top of the heap does all the important work and gets all the glory. There's no provision for learning because the Dinosaur Brain can't learn.

The "Captain Kirk" style leader fights his way to power or, in many cases, starts the company. He or she spends a long time making expensive mistakes before developing a firm hand on the wheel. Such leaders always say, "Sure, I delegate" and they do, but it's always the day-to-day work that they have no interest in. Who always leads the expeditions to the interesting new planets?

What these leaders never delegate is authority. It all stays clipped to their belts, right next to the phaser.

The only way to learn how to use power is to have some. Crew members on the Enterprise get none.

The episodes of "Star Trek" were usually designed to leave the viewer pondering questions of morality or ethics. In that spirit, I'd like to leave you with a question to think about. What would happen if you were on vacation and Romulans attacked your company?

24

The Mentor Relationship

A fledgling tyrannosaurus peers uncertainly into the strange new jungle, alive with the hostile stares of alien lizards. Briefcase tucked under her foreleg, she begins to hack her way alone through the tangled grapevines. Will she take the wrong turn? Will she be ambushed and barbecued by the other dinosaurs? Won't anybody show her the way?

It can be tough to learn the survival skills of your particular corporate jungle. Mentors can help. They can teach you the unwritten rules for behavior and success in your company, things like who has the real clout, how decisions are made, why you shouldn't leave the office before the boss goes home, or where to get a good power lunch these days. Mentors can use their influence to teach you and help you move forward.

The mentor relationship may be beneficial, but it isn't magic. It takes work. Business books are nearly unanimous in telling men and women to find a mentor, someone older who will advise and support them and help them move up. They offer advice on how to pick the right mentor: Should it be someone in your department, another department, or a retiree? Each has different performance and handling characteristics, like a Saab or a BMW. However, these books seldom discuss the motivation of the mentor or the price of having one.

The mentor regards you as an extension of him- or herself. All of your actions reflect on his or her career. If you are involved in a mentor relationship, you need to understand what's in it for the mentor, what he or she will gain by helping you. If you've never thought of that, sit down and do it now. This is not a casual involvement.

The typical view is of the mentor as a selfless old dinosaur who smooths your career path just for the glory of seeing you succeed. That's a very cordial view, and it may not be totally false. Your success is his or her success. It can be a real plus in your mentor's career to have groomed a few young department heads, not bad support in that big push to CEO. But having taken a screw-up under the wing can also be an albatross around the neck.

The results and advantages of the relationship, as well as the who, how and why of choosing a mentor, have been amply discussed. But the rules of the relationship itself are rarely mentioned. From the mentor's point of view, the relationship is usually clearly based on dominance. One thing is certain. The mentor is the dominant dinosaur, and that will never change. What that means exactly is open to discussion, but is seldom discussed. The bottom line is loyalty. "Ask not what your mentor can do for you, but what you can do for your mentor."

Your cortex must be involved at each stage because people are not really programmed for a mentor relationship. The structures for it usually are based on parent-child or courtship roles.

When the two of you are establishing a working bond, think in terms of a contract. The good old question, "What would you like me to do?" is important to ask in this situation. Listen to the answer carefully, because then you will get the contract as stated. It isn't a good idea to blindly accept the mentor's parental role, especially if the mentor seems overbearing from the beginning.

It takes work to develop a mentor relationship like the ones described in the books, and commitment goes both ways.

If you are a mentor, consider what you expect from the relationship. Unless you do this consciously, you can end up with vague emotional ties that grow and, as they do in families, result in guilt, anger and expectations that are never discussed.

Sexual Tensions

Without clear boundaries, the mentor relationship often follows the patterns of a sexual relationship, especially when a man is a woman's mentor and vice versa. Both parties must realize that if there are sexual feelings, they are not to be acted on, although they can be discussed. This falls into the same situation as a doctor-patient or attorney-client relationship, where acting on sexual feelings, if they exist, would exploit the obvious difference in dominance.

Sex should not be the important issue here, yet a very typical form of mentor relationship resembles an affair. Like a successful romance, the involvement must be monogamous, long-term and mutually understood, with the ground rules stated at the beginning. The sexual rules must be clear from the outset.

In a large corporation the idea of mentors really caught on. The company set up a mixer for a crop of new managers, many of whom were women, to meet and get to know the senior people with the aim of creating mentor relationships. The company didn't use the term "mixer," but that's what it was.

Since people didn't really understand the rules for these professional connections, they substituted the better-known patterns for an affair. Of course, that's what many of them became: affairs between older, dominant men and younger, deferential women. The mentor program had to be stopped at this company because of protests from so many executives' wives.

A mentor can be a senior manager in your corporation or an expert in your field, a former boss or perhaps a favorite professor. Mentors don't necessarily have to work in your company, but they must have connections with your company.

Whoever your mentor is, the rules of the relationship must be clear and followed by both parties. A mentor is someone with whom you are working to achieve specific goals. He or she may be a confidant, but is not a lover, a therapist, a parent or a shoulder to cry on.

Connie had gotten a late start in her working life and she was determined to make up for lost time. She was the mother of three young children when she went back to school to get her degree, and she became a stand-out student at the small college she chose. One of her professors, who particularly admired her energy and ambition, pulled strings to get her into a coveted intern program at a local company. After Connie's graduation, that company hired her full time at an entry-level position.

A grateful Connie kept in touch with the professor, a woman slightly older than she, calling frequently to check in, sending notes or cards "just to say I'm thinking of you." The professor was flattered at first that Connie had chosen her as a mentor, but she gradually became irritated by the relationship.

Connie would call to ask for professional and personal advice, then ignore everything the more experienced woman suggested. Every few weeks an impatient Connie would whine that she wasn't being given the choice assignments or complain that nobody would promote her. When her mentor tried to explain that paying your dues means working longer than three months, Connie wouldn't listen.

As her work grew more frustrating, Connie's personal life became chaotic. She would appear, unannounced and in tears, on the professor's doorstep, expecting tea and three hours of sympathy. The mentor felt manipulated into becoming Connie's mother, a role she did not want and would not accept. Connie's outbursts embarrassed her and violated the professional standards the professor thought Connie had learned in her classes. The next time Connie called, the exasperated professor told her to grow up, wait her turn and find a new mom.

The price of having a mentor is similar to the price of having a parrot. You have to listen to the bird whether you want to hear what it has to say or not.

The giving of advice in a mentor relationship is very serious. If you ask your mentor for advice, take it or apologize for not doing so.

Never, ever poll other people. This is a slap in your mentor's face or a signal that the relationship is at an end. An ex-mentor can become an enemy. If you need a second opinion, seek it with the mentor's knowledge and explain very carefully why you can't make the decision based on his or her advice alone.

It is likewise insulting if you demand equal billing with your mentor or expect him or her to treat you as an equal. You can't be an equal with your mentor. The relationship involves doing things his or her way. Your role requires showing some deference, paying attention to your mentor's emotional state, for example, sending a card on his or her birthday, and calling at least once every two weeks. If you aren't willing to pay these respects, then having a mentor is not necessarily your right.

The Young Dinosaur Rebels

The rebellion occurs once the younger person has been in the relationship, gotten his or her sea legs and wants to strike out on his or her own. Then comes the pain involved in emancipation. Mentor relationships are hard to get out of, but sometimes, in order to progress, it's necessary to leave.

An ex-mentor can be an extremely powerful enemy, one with a grudge against you. Many times I have seen someone who was taken under a mentor's wing flourish, until he or she decided to go it alone and began to take stands against the mentor. The mentor then behaved with irrational anger and tried to destroy the career that he had helped to create.

Brett, a bright young executive, was having personality difficulties with his boss. Brett was now sales manager, and his boss was the district vice president. When Brett had entered the company, he had been a sales rep and his mentor was the sales manager, who had taken Brett under his wing and taught him everything he knew. They became friendly and developed what was clearly a mentor relationship.

Things went well for several years, until they both moved up in the organization. When Brett, as sales manager, felt he should be able to make more independent decisions, the mentor felt he'd been forgotten because he wasn't being consulted and his advice wasn't needed. He reacted with his Dinosaur Brain, treating Brett with sarcasm and criticism whenever they met at meetings.

This pattern is completely predictable and is the price you pay for early support. Accepting someone for a mentor means accepting that he or she is dominant. While it's possible to treat a mentor as dominant and still make some of your own decisions, you have to be subtle about it. Follow the suggestions in Chapter 5 for dealing with dominant dinosaurs, and remember that a mentor isn't always totally self-sacrificing or indulgent.

Brett's problem was very much like a teenager's leaving home. A father usually is the last person an 18-year-old would consult, and that's what the situation was here. Brett was trying to get out of the mentor relationship without realizing what the real conflict was. His former mentor was behaving like an abandoned father.

We solved Brett's problem by having him go back in memory to his own adolescence and remember when he left home for college and how he developed a working relationship with his father. Some of the things he did with his father—going back for advice, always showing respect, paying attention to his feelings—were the appropriate ways to treat his ex-mentor.

At what point do you and your mentor become two equal adults? Probably never. If you ever do reach that state, it's important to work out very explicitly what control still exists when you go back for advice.

When You Want to Leave the Nest

It isn't enough for you to decide that you've outgrown the relationship. Being considered an adult in the company will depend a great deal on the mentor's own maturity and possessiveness. That might be a factor in your choice of mentor.

Most of us are still involved in establishing an adult relationship with our parents for as long as they live. Usually we aren't particularly successful. Freud said that a person is not really mature until both of his parents are dead.

To some people, perhaps including your mentor, you remain a child. If your definition of professional maturity means that everyone in the company acknowledges you as an adult, you will be in for some misery.

The criteria must be clear between you and your mentor. When can you grow up? The mentor must be alert for signs of adolescent rebellion and realize that this is normal, although it will be stormy for awhile. The mentor also must provide a certain amount of respect and autonomy to help both of you make the transition.

When Josh was transferred to his department, Roy soon recognized that the younger man had management potential. He assigned Josh to special projects that had high visibility within the company and talked him up to the CEO whenever he could. Josh responded eagerly to Roy's sponsorship and began to treat him as a mentor, dropping in at his office to chat and ask for advice, imitating his business style and putting in extra hours. Roy was pleased at Josh's progress and thought Josh was satisfied too.

The era of good feeling ended the day that Josh was up for a promotion, a job that Roy knew Josh was not yet ready to handle. Because he felt an obligation, Roy nonetheless recommended Josh, as well as one of his more experienced staffers for the post. The senior staffer got the job, and Josh decided it was time to find a new mentor.

"There was only so much I could do for him," Roy said sadly later. "I thought if I could provide more interesting work for him to do, that would be enough for him. Obviously it wasn't, and he decided I didn't have enough clout to help him get where he wanted to go."

The two men handled the transition by maintaining a polite distance for awhile, until Josh got the transfer to a different department that he requested. His career remains at a plateau, but Josh doesn't blame Roy for the standstill. Roy, for his part, wishes Josh well but can't help feeling a little disappointed in his protege's unrealistic expectations for their relationship.

25

Why People Get Involved in Office Romances

Why do people get romantically involved at work in the first place? Love still makes the world go 'round, and where else would someone be more likely to meet Mr. or Ms. Right than at the office? Working on a project together, then meeting for a few innocent conversations over coffee can suddenly blossom into something more. Something nobody intended. An office affair.

Far too many romances between colleagues are completely unintended. Falling in love is too important to allow it to happen by accident, yet that's how most office romances begin. Why?

As we discovered in Chapter 7, human courtship follows instinctive patterns that are based in the Dinosaur Brain. When these stages occur in a high school, everybody seems to know what they mean. When they happen at work, people don't recognize them as easily, especially when one or both parties are married.

People see what they want to see. They can end up feeling that they had no choice about getting involved until it was too late. In this chapter, we consider why office affairs begin, then we review some ways to distinguish between The Real Thing and "just another office romance."

Not all affairs between co-workers are bad, but the dangers involved are formidable. In the beginning, an office romance seems so right. In its early stages it can give the lovers the extra energy and confidence they need to lose ten pounds or go for that promotion. Only later, when the excitement wears off and the complications set in, do they begin to wonder, "How did I get into this in the first place?"

Familiarity

We're most likely to fall in love with the people who are physically closest to us every day. It's literally true that the most likely place to find Ms. Right or Ms. Wrong is at the office. When two people work closely together, share the same problems and confide in each other—Dinosaur Brains being what they are—it's easy to press for more from the relationship.

Office romances are also an expression of a real need. Our jobs are very important to us, and it's great to have someone to talk to who really understands. Especially in the beginning, most office romances aren't grounded in sexual needs but in the need to be understood and appreciated.

Let's face it. Most of us are more lovable at work than we are anywhere else. We tend to like ourselves better at the office than at home. We're more in control and more confident. We're doing what we know how to do and being paid for it.

The familiarity we have with colleagues is more controlled and limited than our closeness to the people at home. It's easier to show the best side of our personality at work and to keep our less charming traits a secret. For instance, how many of your co-workers, who see you suavely spearing scampi during expense-account lunches, know you enjoy a dinner of peanut butter licked from a knife, Doritos and beer at home? And have your colleagues, who compliment you on your power-look career suits, ever gotten a close-up look at you in your typical weekend couture: a centuries-old flannel shirt and baggy sweatpants?

Work also gives people something to talk about at the beginning, until they get to know each other. If you've ever been on a first date, you know how important that is.

Office romances can start because there's a strong bonding effect when colleagues go through the same professional highs and lows. More of these affairs start in bad times than good, because it's natural to seek companionship when times are hard—to talk things over or just to suffer together in silence.

Often, through the intercession of the Dinosaur Brain, strong emotions that began in the conference room can lead to strong emotions that end in the bedroom.

Status is also an issue in attraction. The Dinosaur Brain is quite keen on the office politics of dominance and hierarchies. People, responding to this pattern, feel flattered when someone higher above them on the corporate ladder pays attention to them romantically. They can become involved in an affair, often to discover later that they have been sexually harassed.

Safety

Next to familiarity, the biggest reason office romances begin is that they offer deceptive safety from the conflicting pressures of career versus personal life. It's easy to believe that, if you are involved with someone who works with you, there will be no conflict. Surely a colleague (and lover) will understand if you have to work late. Certainly there will be no hassle if you skip the Saturday matinee and go to the office "just for a few minutes." And who would be more likely to sympathize if you're too tired for sex because of pressure from work?

Maybe a lover (and colleague) will be understanding at the beginning of a relationship, but never at the end.

A significant number of office romances can and do turn into The Real Thing. So far no one in the laboratory or elsewhere can say what factors guarantee a long-lasting and satisfying relationship. Love is something that is finally not understandable, but there are some guidelines and caveats to help determine whether this is The Real Thing or just another office romance:

1. Try to predict the future. How will the relationship fit with your life and career? Where will the conflicts be? Imagine where the relationship and your life and career will be a year from now. If you think they'll remain stable and exactly as they are now, you're probably engaging in wishful thinking.

2. Know the next step in the courtship ritual, the next level of intimacy, and think hard about what the future holds if you take that step. (Refer to Chapter 7 for a complete explanation of each stage of the typical office courtship.)

Ask yourselves, What do we want? What kind of relationship is it going to be? Casual sex, a good time and no regrets later? A supportive and sexual friendship, with no strings attached? A long-term commitment?

3. If one of you has a history of other office romances, keep your guard up.

What do you do if each of you has different ideas? If one person is thinking "fling," and the other is thinking "marriage," there can be trouble.

A romance can end in friendship if you agree that your wants are just too dissimilar. But if you can't agree on where you want the relationship to go, and the relationship still doesn't end, we're talking crimes of passion, which are inappropriate at most jobs.

4. If one of you is married, the probability of a successful relationship drops greatly. You're faced with some really tough choices. You both have to decide where you stand in terms of morality, commitment and secrecy, to name just a few. If you pretend that your lover's spouse doesn't exist, you'll get caught, and the painful questions will become even more painful.

It's also important to realize that there's a good chance that your lover eventually will treat you in the same way that his or her spouse was treated.

If one of you has been separated or divorced within the past six months, the odds also drop for making the relationship a success. There are still too many changes to process, too many adjustments to make and too many false starts to attempt before The Real Thing is likely to come along.

5. Be alert for signs of denial—pretending nobody else knows about this—in yourself or the other person. If you're having a relationship, you can be pretty sure that somebody knows or suspects. Denial means you're quite skillful at ignoring large doses of reality when you're deciding how to behave, and this is never a good sign.

6. Is one person doing most of the giving? If so, what is expected in return? If someone is building up obligations, the prognosis is not good. Lack of reciprocation is also a negative sign.

7. If you haven't talked about exclusivity and possessiveness and set explicit rules, beware.

8. Ask yourself if either of you is using the relationship as medication to fight depression or burnout. If a relationship is what gets you up and in to work in the morning, that relationship is suspect. You're using a Dinosaur Brain pattern, an overdose of emotion, to distract yourself from a very real problem that needs to be solved. Many people are adrenaline junkies, and the constant, daily involvement of the Dinosaur Brain can indicate they're not very happy with their jobs.

9. Can you both say "No"? Is there compromise? If there are no disagreements, beware. Real people, who aren't holding back, sometimes disagree. If there are disagreements, compromises and real changes on major issues, that's a very good sign.

10. Most important, are promises made and kept? The secret to The Real Thing is commitment. Both people have to be willing to make promises and keep them, no matter how hard it becomes. Does your lover keep promises to others? If not, what makes you think you'll be treated differently?

11. Check out your feelings with a trusted friend, and give him or her permission to offer a real opinion. Or seek professional advice. Believe what you hear! If you find yourself coming up with reasons why your friend or a counselor doesn't really understand what's going on, or why this relationship is different, it's time to back off.

12. If one of you drinks or uses drugs to excess, all bets are off. Often this type of person has a great deal of charm. Many people tend to fall for alcoholics, feeling that the alcoholic would change if there were just somebody who understood. This is seldom the case, and people who are abusers of alcohol or drugs also tend to draw disastrous relationships like magnets. If you find yourself interested in someone who has a substance abuse problem, it's time to rethink the situation. Quickly.

26

How to Save Yourself If Your Company Is "One Big Happy Family"

When I hear somebody describe his or her company as one big happy family, I generally know I'm talking to Dad. He's happy because the company is structured to make him happy at the expense of everybody else. It's also possible that I'm talking to a favorite uncle, or even a long-suffering, loyal mom, but Dad is the one with the really big smile.

The basic rules for hierarchies are programmed into our Dinosaur Brains, but detailed instructions for our particular roles are usually supplied by the hierarchy into which we were born. There is no way to stop people from playing out their family roles at the office. This is especially true in family-owned businesses.

Is a family like a business and can it be run that way? I'm going to opt for the psychologist's prerogative and answer yes and no. Yes, if it's run like a functional family; no, if it's like the crazy families most of us grew up in.

All too often the family patterns in business are elaborations on Dinosaur Brain themes that people lapse into when they don't think. People who don't think about what they're doing almost always get into trouble. There is a big difference between adopting a family role as a management style and falling into one because that's the only thing you know how to do. Management is far too important a task to be done on automatic pilot.

Companies don't usually act like healthy, functional families, in which people's roles are flexible and less stereotyped, children are allowed to grow up, and family members talk about conflicts and make compromises with one another. People from such families can grow out of their roles and do not need to play the same roles for the rest of their lives.

The big happy family patterns that occur in business usually are the patterns of dysfunctional or unhealthy families. Here, the important remains unsaid, especially about very abnormal behaviors. These family roles tend to be stereotyped, and people feel as if there is no possibility of behaving in any other way.

These unhealthy patterns are much harder to grow out of; they are transferred to business more often than healthy ones. People who grew up in dysfunctional families, such as those in which there was an abusive or alcoholic parent, tend to see every new problem as a restatement of the basic unsolved problem from the past and usually try to solve them with the same inadequate tools. Even when a corporate family is really bizarre, they hardly even notice. They just stay on and try to get by as best they can, just as they did at home.

Corporate Family Examples

Following are several examples of corporate families, described in terms of stereotypic roles, and suggestions for saving yourself if you find yourself in any of these kinds of systems. I'll leave it to you to decide whether they're happy.

The Moralistic Patriarch

R. L. Johnson, the head of finance, believes that the problem with this country is that people no longer adhere to the old-fashioned values. All of his business meetings open with a devotion, and everyone in his department must wear a little flag in his or her lapel. The meetings involve very little talking about business; usually R. L. gives a lecture on a moral issue, such as the work ethic, or the divorce or alcohol problem of a member of another department. R. L. always comes up with verses from the Scriptures and talks about how his people can prevent terrible things like this from happening to them.

Advancement in R. L.'s department seems to come by holding a similar value system to his, rather than ability to do the work. In fact, ability seems a real hindrance to promotion at times. Morality and frugality are his bottom lines. R. L.'s management techniques would be more appropriate in a rural dry goods store than a multinational corporation, but anybody who disagrees is quickly shown the door.

What do you do in this situation?

1. *Decide if you can live with it, because you can't change it.* You'll never get anywhere being the rebellious teenager, casting down your flag pin, demanding that you be judged on your professional merits or pointing to business journal articles about how this work should be done. People like R. L. are firm in their moral values, and not even God himself could shake their beliefs.

There is no point in blowing up over this. Once you realize you're in this environment, you can either accept it or get out. You probably won't be able to start a revolution. You must decide if you can live with a double standard: Subscribe to the corporate line while you're there, and take off your flag pin when you leave.

2. *Realize that for this system to operate, someone somewhere must be running the show.* A company or division cannot be run as a religious sect; it will quickly run into the ground. Usually there is a power behind the patriarch who is actually taking care of business. If you want to exist within this system, you need to find him or her. It might be a select committee or, if the person is really Machiavellian, he might not want his identity to be known.

If you can find the person behind the throne, he or she is definitely the one to get close to. This protection is the only kind that is real and that's worth anything. Don't rely on competence to save you. In such a system, competence is minor. Being a card-carrying party member is the major issue.

3. *Expect rewards and punishments that are not commensurate with behavior.* The patriarch sees rewards as gifts from God and punishment as retribution for offenses such as thought-crimes. These people often cover their sadism with the justification that they are "sending a message."

4. *Consider getting out and set an orderly goal for leaving.* You could just pick a fight and get fired. It's best, however, to plan a short-term career goal, accomplish it and leave with a good recommendation. Express gratitude, thank R.L. for saving your soul, but tell him your true calling is elsewhere.

When you go to your next job (or to a job interview), don't point out how insane the situation was because you never know what kind of a dinosaur you're talking to. Your prospective employer will probably consider any complaints about R. L., no matter how valid, as the kind of thing you'll be saying about him next.

The All-American, Situation-Comedy Parent

June is a nice person and she runs a nice department. She values harmony and cooperation and absolutely refuses to believe there could be anything else. Don't come to her with a problem, especially if it involves emotions and personal disagreements. She'll tell you that a positive attitude always wins. Secretly, she may be giving you a black mark. June sometimes believes in killing the messenger who brings bad tidings. Her department is one big happy family, and mother does know best.

June probably represents this country's most common management style, and it's not altogether dysfunctional, as long as the manager pays attention to important problems instead of sweeping everything under the rug. Typically, the emotional conflicts are ignored. If they're major ones that don't go away and that come back to haunt people, then this type of manager has a problem—and so do you if you work for someone like her. Here's what to do:

1. *Realize that bosses like June have a very limited tolerance for problems.* Have your own priorities straight, and ask her to take on one issue at a time. Make sure that you start from the top. Don't try to warm her up on the little stuff.

2. *Develop a plan for presenting the issue.* Have your information at hand, and remember to gather more facts than feelings.

3. *To get this person's ear, never come with complaints; come with a plan for making things better.* Don't say, "There's a problem here, June." Instead, try, "There's an area where we can make some improvements; here's my plan. . . ."

People who tend to act like rebellious teenagers (see Chapter 27) tend to hate managers like June. Often someone will move into the position of "mother" below June in the hierarchy and try to take responsibility for all the aches and pains of the children.

Corporate Mother

If they only knew the long hours Bill has spent protecting them, the department heads wouldn't be so angry at him all the time. True, the chairman seems to be off in his own grandiose world a lot, traveling. When he returns, his whims, his insistence on immediate changes and radical schemes for saving money or getting written up in management magazines—all of these things have to be shaped into workable business. This is when Bill slaves the hardest, persuading, cajoling, sometimes even begging. If they only knew. Why are they always so angry? They obviously want Bill gone, but why? Don't they know how much worse it could be without him?

The corporate mother's role is to screen the father from difficulties and protect him from things that might make him angry. The theory is that the mother is protecting the children from the father's wrath. This situation can happen when the boss is the father-knows-best kind, a moralistic patriarch, an alcoholic or otherwise dysfunctional in some way.

The mother definitely does not have to be a woman. He or she is torn between loyalties to the father and the kids. At best, these emotions are self-destructive; at worst, they enable and perpetuate just the kind of craziness he or she is trying to protect against.

In most companies that operate this way, people get angry at Mom for standing between them and Dad or transfer some of their anger at Dad to the more accessible Mom.

The only answer is for Mom to back off. The situation will never change as long as the corporate father is isolated from the kids and not accountable to the company family for his actions. If you're in this position, consider taking an extended vacation, a transfer or working on an independent project. This will be difficult for you if you define your role as indispensable, standing in the way of certain tragedy. Let the tragedy come. It will be better for everybody in the long run.

Mother figures are often very good people, working very hard at an impossible task. Many of them feel their job is their home and there is nowhere else for them to go. Often they are talented and capable and could do much better in a different job with different responsibilities.

The Dark Mother

Nobody can predict Pat's moods. If he's feeling good, the office is bright and sunny, but if he's feeling bad, the tiniest offense can bring a torrent of yelling or, worse, the Silent Treatment. You can get on his hit list for no particular reason, and if you're on it, you'll hear about a lot of things that Pat says behind your back.

Pat is competent, but he's difficult to work with. He has problems at home and is under a lot of pressure from the boss and the market. He seems to delegate his stress to his underlings and inadvertently creates more stress for himself. His unpredictability is a good screening device; it protects him from the terror of the unknown. Pat is always pumped up and reacting emotionally, so people tend to protect him.

This style is not fun for Pat. He's not doing it because he enjoys it. Rather, he is always worried about something and always taking some sort of impulsive action about what worries him. Managers like Pat are almost always using their Dinosaur Brains, and if you know that, then you know a good deal about how to cope with them.

1. *Avoid the temptation to communicate indirectly*, as Pat does. Forget whatever you hear about what he has said behind your back. The people who bear these tales are not your friends and are not trying to help you. Nor should you pay any attention to the "confidences" that Pat makes to you. He will deny them later and is just asking you to get in on his indirect communication system.

2. *Deal with him directly*. A good style of doing this is to say, "Pat, when you said . . ., I felt. . . . Is that what you intended?"

People like Pat usually don't fire anyone or do irreparable harm to your career. They tend to goad people into leaving. If you deal directly with him, expect a lot of petty attacks but nothing really big. It depends on how much you can take. You'll know you're winning if you hear all kinds of stories behind your back.

Probably the worst that could happen is that Pat will try to arrange to have you transferred to another department, and that's not so bad.

3. *Try flattery*. Realize that people like Pat are using their Dinosaur Brains so much of the time that they're very undiscriminating about emotional issues. They are extremely susceptible to compliments, so if you want to get their ear, you can use flattery so bald-faced that you wouldn't believe an intelligent person could fall for it.

You can use what I call the Bugs Bunny strategy, which I discovered while watching a Bugs Bunny cartoon in which a big bruiser was about to pound Bugs to a pulp. Bugs looked at him and said, "Hey, doc, show me that profile. Was you ever in the movies? You've sure got the face for it." Immediately the thug was posing and grinning and lapping it up.

Of course, Bugs had the chance to get away at that point, but he stayed around long enough to make the big bruiser look pretty silly. Believe it or not, this level of flattery will work with a person like Pat. It can save you from humiliation or unpleasant behavior, and you can use it to get special favors, if that's what you want.

Eccentric Uncles and Favorite Sons

Often when a company has an erratic or dysfunctional boss, such as the ones I've described, there is another person in the picture, someone with knowledge in an area in which the boss is not an expert. This person is touted as an expert, although many times he is not an expert at all. Very often he is a fiscal-type officer, whose main qualification is that he provides justification for the top lizard to do whatever he wants. This person usually commands top dollar and is really a high-level flunkie.

There seem to be two types of people in this position. One is the eccentric uncle, whose knowledge of fiscal issues is about twenty years out of date. He can be blustery and persuasive. He is loyal to the boss and only to the boss.

The other type is usually somebody bright and ambitious, maybe fresh out of business or law school, who sees this position as a quick way to gain power.

If you're out to take on one of these father-figure bosses, one of these two may be his Achilles heel. The eccentric uncle or favorite son is the one who will usually make the objective mistake; he is set up to take the risk for the father. A beleaguered father will throw this person to the lizards in a last-ditch effort to save himself. Uncle's high salary really pays for this, rather than for his expertise.

Sometimes people don't realize that they're being interviewed for this kind of position. If you are facing a situation like this, talk to the last person who had the job. Find out exactly what was expected and what the job duties involved. Eccentric uncles and favorite sons must know that, even if they support the father's system whole-heartedly, they'll be the ones who take the fall.

Saving Yourself in a Not-So-Happy Corporate Family

Some confusion of family and business roles can be found in virtually any company. Our Dinosaur Brains give us the basic hierarchical pattern, and our personal family experiences tell us, "Don't upset your father." Often this situation creates confusion. People wonder, as they did growing up, "Is this normal?" "Do I have a right to feel bad in this family?" "Is it me or them?" Needless to say, this leads to wasted effort, stress and frustration.

The big difference between functional and dysfunctional companies is that the functional ones can talk about what's happening. The corporate structure does not isolate people from the consequences of their actions.

If the structure in your company is particularly pathological or rigid, you might need the services of a corporate family therapist (commonly called organizational development consultants). In most companies, however, you can talk about these issues in a rational, planned way.

The strategy for the situation-comedy parent works best. Focus on your priorities and on what you want to happen, rather than pointing out all the bad things that are going on. Most of us are programmed to deal with this kind of conflict by just pretending the situation is OK and we're inadequate, or by acting like angry teenagers or dinosaurs vying for power. When we aren't ignoring it, we tend to think in terms of starting a revolution or going public with the news about how bad things are, or just getting together and griping about it. Tattling is never a constructive action unless there are crimes being committed.

The way to talk about the situation is coolly, with the cortex. Decide what you want; deal with one issue at a time. If there are people in your corporation who are isolating top management, try to get on their good sides. Try to persuade them to agree to more open meetings where you can talk with the people upstairs. The only way to save yourself if your company is one big happy family is to let it be known that some people aren't really all smiles.

27

Corporate Juvenile Delinquents

Ever notice how each year's new crop of employees seems younger and younger? They certainly seem less mature than you were at their age, and they surely don't seem to work as hard as you did. As for showing respect, well, forget it.

By the way, do you remember all the promises you made to yourself when you were low person on the totem pole about how you were going to treat your juniors when you got up there? Are you keeping those promises? If not, I'm sure you have your reasons. One of the best has to do with the characteristic behaviors of people who are approaching maturity.

When we're talking about young people in corporations, we're speaking in a relative sense, of course. Usually teenagers don't start out in executive positions, but most people who are new in the company or in new positions act like teenagers because that's the role they know. They're outsiders, and somehow they must figure out the rules for becoming insiders.

Young people and young dinosaurs have always acted the same: pushing, shoving, fighting, preening and trampling other people in their never-ending battle for independence and dominance. Corporate teenagers, like any other adolescents, develop their identities by testing the limits of the system by rebelling and talking back. They're saying, in essence, "I have a right to express myself in my own way, whether you like it or not." They begin their quest for identity by questioning authority and then by trying to think for themselves.

Basically, these are normal, predictable and time-limited behaviors, but they can be irritating and frustrating to the corporate parental figures, and if they last too long they are not in the teenagers' best interests. Some people manage to stay teenagers until retirement time.

If senior management defines this normal behavior as juvenile delinquency (an out-of-date term and an out-of-date way of thinking) there is bound to be war. Management cannot win this kind of war. Sympathy will always be with the "wronged" teenager. You may get rid of a troublemaker, but it costs a lot of bad press.

Adolescents of any sort can be direct, to-the-point and creative. They question authority and challenge the established order. In many cases, authority deserves to be questioned. Even the brightest and best of us old folks get into ruts in our thinking.

The bad part is the rebel-without-a-cause syndrome: rebellion for rebellion's sake, even when it's self-destructive. Our country honors adolescence seemingly above all else. The United States was built on rebellion and self-determination. All of our greatest heroes seem to have some component of the overgrown teenager. We like the freshness, and we admire the rebels, but, boy, are they a problem to supervise.

Let's look at how to deal with some typical kinds of corporate juvenile delinquents.

Job versus Career

Marie wants everything that's coming to her, and she gets it. She was hired right out of one of the best business schools in the country, and she's very bright. She gives the company her all for eight hours a day, but after that, she goes home. The rest of her life is important too. All the magazines say so. She takes all of her vacations exactly when they're scheduled because they are her right. Marie says if you don't look out for yourself, nobody else will do it for you.

She fights hard for the people in her department, but anybody else can go take a flying leap. She has gotten a couple of promotions because her hiring agreement said she would have a chance to move up. She gets raises regularly because she demands them.

Lately Marie has been quite angry with her boss because she was passed over for a big promotion, and this wasn't the first time, either. She has mumbled a few things about the Old Boy network and the possibility of a discrimination suit. She may get her promotion eventually; she may even win her lawsuit, but she will never get to the top.

Marie has defined her territory as herself and her department alone. She doesn't seem to have any loyalty to the company as a whole, and she isn't willing to sacrifice anything personally to the greater good. People notice that. Nobody says you have to, but people notice when you don't. It's noted when you leave at five o'clock on the dot every day or take a vacation when your department is in the midst of a crisis.

Of course, you have to take care of yourself, but maybe you shouldn't be as vehement as Marie is about it. When there's conflict between the greater good and your own good, you choose yourself if you have a *job*. If you have a *career*, you take the greater good.

Aside from its faults, the essence of the Old Boy network is that privilege has its obligations. The outsiders see all of the privileges; the insiders see the obligations. Marie demanded the privileges but felt that she had already paid her dues. Too bad, Marie.

If you supervise someone like Marie, you cannot demand that he or she share your value system. Choosing a job over a career probably runs counter to your own values, but that doesn't mean it's wrong.

It's most important to let people know specifically how your company defines the difference between job and career. You can point out that options are limited for people who choose to define their work as a job. If they do well, they can be promoted, but only so high.

One of the best ways is by pointing out the people who are rewarded with promotions and asking, "How is this person's behavior different from yours?" Be ready with specific examples, such as, "In this situation you demanded a raise and she asked for more responsibility" or "He volunteered for the following projects, and you left at five every day."

Rebel Without a Cause

Dave knows that management is out to get him. He's been passed by for two promotions, and he knows exactly what he can get away with now. He has little hope of advancement, so his idea is just screw them before they screw him. Everybody knows what Dave thinks of the company. You'd think he would try for a job where he could have more success, but Dave thinks the company owes him, and he's going to get everything he deserves. He's just putting in his time until he can cash in on that great pension system.

The best way to deal with a person like Dave is to have started years ago, explaining the company's goals and objectives, employee evaluations and the system of rewards and promotions. Then Dave's energies could have been directed, and he wouldn't be so bitter now. Once the damage is done, it is very hard, but not impossible, to win him over, so try that first.

An incredible number of people like Dave are in the corporate system because people are rewarded more often for being in the right place at the right time than for real merits. Most companies have employee ratings and goals and objectives systems, but they often have them because they're fashionable, and they don't check to see how or if they're really being used.

The only solution to most situations such as the one with Dave is to isolate him. Give him a promotion to a position where he's doing something he likes to do and is of value to the company but doesn't require much interaction with subordinates. The worst thing you can do is to leave him as a line manager, where his ideas and stories, plus the natural tendency of teenagers to champion the underdog, could turn him into a folk hero.

Better yet, if you can give him his early retirement, do it. He'll be happy and you'll be happy. You cannot afford to start a war with someone like Dave. He can sue you, make you look bad or become a martyr, and all of these things will cost you. When you have a rebel without a cause like Dave, your Dinosaur Brain could be screaming, "Kill him!" but your cortex needs to say, "Go out of your way to be fair to him." Whatever you do, get him out of the way. He can poison a lot of working relationships.

People like Dave also tend to develop stress-related illnesses. Those who have the biggest problems with stress are those who believe they have the least control over what happens to them. When I go into a company to consult, one of the tricks I use to show how smart I am is to say, "Just from looking at the empty offices and work spaces, I can show you the people who are having troubles with stress and burnout."

How do I do it? I don't look at messy desks; instead I find cartoon calendars—the kind that tell you 365 reasons per year why you're a victim of life. I also look for cute little posters saying, "Hang in there 'til Friday," or work areas decorated with little signs, statues and markers that, if read correctly, say, "I'm not in control of what happens to me. I'm at war with my job. I don't like my work."

The Sick Child

Another kind of juvenile delinquent is the sick child. Of course, there are times when people just get sick. They get the flu, pull their backs out, have a heart attack, develop psychological problems or trouble with alcohol or drugs. The people I'm talking about, however, have a persistent history of illness, often not the same illness. For a few years it might be back problems, for instance, then colitis, then migraines. These people have a pattern of dealing with job stresses by getting sick and being absent from work. They realize that demands on them are eased when they're sick, so they pay more attention to any kind of symptoms.

The way to deal with this is to have a coherent policy about absenteeism. Buying back days that people don't use is a good one. If you do career histories of employees, you can get a clearer idea of the danger signs of overusing sickness and develop policies that relate to the effects of absenteeism.

Another way to deal with the illness problem is to set up illness-prevention and wellness programs within the company. New research points to long-term benefits of such programs as smoking cessation, weight loss, exercise and stress-management. These programs are much more productive than punishing people who are absent too much and tend to work best if they can be prescribed specifically for problem employees.

The best way to handle this situation is to increase the response cost for sickness. Try to make it harder to misuse sick time than it is to come to work. Proscriptive health programs work well, as does requiring a lot of corroborative paperwork if an employee stays out. (Someone like this will always get the papers signed, so it won't prevent absence.) A regular goal of 100 percent attendance can work too.

Avoid taking action that would make it seem that you are punishing people for being sick. There are two very good reasons for this. First, this battle is another you won't win. Sick is sick, and these people usually are not malingering; they really are ill. (Malingerers eventually will run out of doctors.) Second, as always, your best employees judge you by how you treat your worst.

M*A*S*H Units

You know the show: a bunch of intelligent, antiwar doctors are competent and loving. In a crazy situation, they keep themselves sane by acting crazy. You can see M*A*S*H units developing, especially with young, bright, creative people.

Notice the crazy hats, the rude parody of the corporate logo, the graffiti on all the posters, and the strange outfits in the software development department of your company or your own particular M*A*S*H unit. What you're seeing are the behaviors that intelligent, creative people come up with when they feel disenfranchised or under almost intolerable stress.

Behaviors like this are usually positive, though they can be annoying to the people in charge. Of course, the behavior will persist as long as it is annoying, because these corporate teenagers feel that's the only way they can get the ear of the people in power. They delight in being the bad kids.

Often they are people in the research or new-ideas department, and they know very well that they're expendable, that they'll be the first group to be laid off the next time money is short. They do not see themselves as having any kind of career path at all. They're happiest doing their work, not managing people. In our corporate system, people like this are seldom rewarded, although they might be the best and brightest people around.

The usual management response is to punish groups like this by sending out memos about what you can and can't put on the wall or enforcing dress codes and further alienating these people.

The real way to deal with them should be listen to them and make some corporate decisions about their value. New ideas can be your bread and butter, but so many companies force their disenfranchised departments into the behavior of dinosaurs who have been pushed out of the hierarchy. Then the corporate powers use that irreverent behavior as justification for not having these people on a career development path because they're so weird or unstable.

People in M*A*S*H units are usually very popular throughout the company, and it's very easy to make martyrs out of them. The answer is to let them know how they can be heard and how they can gain rewards and job security.

Junior Shark Tank

The younger people in finance spend all their time competing with one another, trying to make each other look stupid. There are only so many slots in management, and it's well known that if you make one mistake, your chances are just about nil. The game involves daring other people to take risks, then doing what you can to make them blow it. Promotions tend to go to the people who are most ruthless or most cautious, and employees spend a lot of time and effort stabbing others in the back when there is a job to be done.

The way to deal with this systemic problem is to make career paths clear, explain in advance the kinds of behaviors you will reward, and promote people who act like leaders and do responsible work, rather than tattle-tales and back-stabbers.

Often you'll find a department like this is headed by an older dinosaur who sets the behavior pattern for his juniors. If you have a shark-tank situation, look at the person who's doing the feeding.

If you're the new person who's moved in to get control of a shark-infested situation, one of the best approaches is to set up orderly competitions, in which you state a problem and offer rewards for people who can come up with the best solutions. Give people projects to work on, independently or in groups of three or four. Make sure that there is no way a single person can get his or her name on any part of the group's project. Success and rewards go to people who do teamwork, rather than to individual stars who screw the competition.

Usually the problems of corporate juvenile delinquents are problems within the system. No teenager in existence, either the corporate or the family kind, ever responded to and changed behavior because of a parental lecture. Instead, if you can give people clear directions and set up your systems to encourage and reward maturity, maturity is what you'll get. If you're secretly rooting for the bad guys, however, then they're the ones who will win.

Most of all, see what kinds of behaviors have been of past value to your company and make sure your structure is set up to reward those. Have your corporate historian, who serves some of the cortical functions for the company, trace the career paths of people who joined the company 30 years ago, and see what they were doing at 5, 10, 15 and 20 years. Then take a look at some people who joined the company 20 years ago, 10 years ago and so forth.

If you choose about 25 people at random for each time period, depending on the size of your company, you'll get a pretty good idea of the normal trends, such as how job ratings relate to actual success. For example, you might see that your company is really serving as a training ground for other corporations or that diligence is rewarded.

This way you have facts instead of theory about how the company operates. The idea is catching on in companies. It makes a lot of sense, but is certainly not something the Dinosaur Brain would think up. The Dinosaur Brain would look at the immediate situation and punish someone who did the wrong thing. By actually looking at employees' career paths, you can see what happened to the people who started out as rebels and where they ended up in 20 years. It might be surprising.

28

Dealing with Old Dinosaurs

Being bright, ambitious and very junior is a tough role, but by playing it well, you move up in the hierarchy. Beware of your own instincts and experiences in this situation, however; young dinosaurs are pushy and loud, always trying to advance themselves over others.

Young dinosaurs, like teenagers, are dependent one minute, surly the next. Neither of these behaviors is at all impressive to older dinosaurs. If you really want to move up, you'll have to find a way to make the old dinosaurs think you're intelligent, hard-working and dependable enough to be one of them. Here are some suggestions:

1. *Demonstrate your ability to listen;* don't expect them to listen to you. Many people think the best way to get others to like or promote them is by dazzling them with brilliance and ability. Nobody likes to think somebody junior is brighter or more qualified than he is. Actual studies show that the way to get people to like you is by liking and showing an interest in *them*.

When you get advice, show you can take it. Every old dinosaur has a standard lecture and set of stories. They may be about the decline of the work ethic, for example, or the value of sports in teaching fair play. Whatever they are, listen and refer to them in conversations and reports.

The most impressive thing you can do is add to one of these old dinosaur's truisms. If you can find a quote in which someone like Abraham Lincoln or Henry Ford said the same thing, or if you can cite facts and figures that support the dinosaur's standard stories, nothing—not grades, ideas or recommendations—will make him think more highly of your intelligence and ability.

The boss's idea of intelligence is someone who listens to him, and, believe me, there is usually something to listen to. If you close your mind and say to yourself, "It's just the same old stuff," you're likely to miss something important, even if it's just the chance to know how more senior people think.

If the old dinosaur points his finger in the air a lot when he talks, or repeats the same line again and again, you can be sure that he values being listened to. These oratorical behaviors are signs that he thinks what he is saying is very important. If you want him to think you're smart, act as if you consider it important too.

2. *Be friendly.* This applies to your dealings both with old dinosaurs and with your own age-mates. Meet as many old dinosaurs as you can. It's a good idea to ask someone to introduce you. Be sure to demonstrate to the old lizard that you know his name and legend. Say something like, "You're Mike Goldberg, the man behind the Wonder Widget. We talked about that development project in business school."

Pay particular attention to smiling, which has a number of different meanings. Usually it's seen as a sign of friendliness. You should smile occasionally at people both above and below you. Studies show that from the earliest ages, women smile more than men. In general, men need to learn to smile more and women, less.

Smiling when you're anxious (it does show) is a sign of deference. This behavior is usually inappropriate with subordinates. If you smile when you're nervous or when you want people to agree with you, every Dinosaur Brain on the block will know more about your internal state than you want him or her to know. Practice other expressions of worry and concern in front of the mirror.

Shyness is usually considered surliness, and nobody likes a surly teenager. Realize that old dinosaurs may be shy too. When you're thrown together at a meeting or lunch, you can try to take the burden of making pleasantries off them. If they don't respond, shut up right away.

All of these ideas apply to your relationships with your age-mates too. People who have good reputations among their peers also will have good reputations with the old dinosaurs. It's good to make as many friends as you can, develop loyalties and make other people look good.

3. *Be reverent.* Demonstrate that you are aware that there are values other than your own personal gain. Show you're a team player. Screwing other people is never good form. Show that you can make sacrifices and defer gratification.

It's also important to be seen as a good citizen. Old dinosaurs like to see themselves as serving. They're usually on the boards of directors of various charities and civic organizations. The poster of a charity that you work for would be a nice addition to your office decor, although it might be a good idea to avoid something that's politically sensitive. If you can save the whales or end world hunger without stridency, that's fine, but remember that nobody likes an Old Testament prophet, especially a young one.

4. *Know when to keep your mouth shut.* Assume you're allowed five questions and one complaint a year. When you do make your yearly complaint, make sure it's in this form: "I would like clearer priorities on this project. Can you provide them?" Don't say, "You don't give me any direction." People who complain are written off and ignored.

Questions have many functions besides being requests for information. They can also be attacks, as in "Didn't you say to put those items under miscellaneous expenses in the budget? Now are you telling me they're to be attributed to my program?"

I know that managers say, "Don't be afraid to ask questions," but even if they say that to you, make sure it's true. Most often employees who ask a lot of questions are seen as lacking initiative. Instead, listen well and then act. It's often better to make a mistake than to ask a lot of questions that really translate into, "Reassure me." People in responsible corporate positions almost universally hate overdependency.

If you made a mistake, say, "I made a mistake and I will do the following to correct it. . . ." Don't explain why you made the mistake, especially if you're going to point the finger at somebody else. It never pays to look defensive. To the Dinosaur Brain, that's asking for attack.

At meetings, consider your words carefully. Don't just ask a question for the sake of having others hear your voice. Pay attention to the number of times you engage in deferential behaviors, such as saying, "That's a good idea" or smiling and nodding. In general, men need to do this more and women less.

Eye contact is always good, except in situations where you might be perceived as attacking. Pointing your eyes down often makes you look like less of a threat.

Know that there are conversations into which you must be invited to join, just as there are tables at which you must be asked to sit.

5. *Be indispensable.* Cultivate a specialty area. Know all you can. Keep up to date. Don't take on the more glamorous areas at which other people already think they are experts. Avoid the easy areas, and choose something that other people consider distasteful or boring.

Federal regulations are a good choice; somebody needs to know them, and most people don't want to be that person. (If you decide to take on federal regulations as a specialty, don't see yourself as a representative of the federal government and start pointing out all the rules that your company is violating. Be there as a resource.)

Another good specialty is anything that involves new technology. Let your expertise be known by quoting authorities in the field rather than quoting your own opinion. At the beginning, commit to a particular theory or approach. Never say, "I'm a generalist or eclectic" until you've had at least 20 years of experience. It's great to know all the approaches, but buy into one.

6. *Be committed.* If you're on the lookout, you can find profundity everywhere. I once opened a fortune cookie that said, "Creativity without discipline is like having wings with no feet." I still have that fortune on the wall in my office. Young dinosaurs must be able to demonstrate that they have endurance, that they can do a good job on what needs to be done and not just on what they like to do. Inspiration is easy; perspiration comes harder.

Do every job you're assigned as if it were a job worth doing, even if it's scut work. Do what you say when you say you'll do it. Never miss the chance to set a deadline for yourself, then meet it. Say, "I'll have it done by. . . ." and make sure you do.

If you're assigned duties that you don't like, do them first. Nothing turns off older dinosaurs faster than hearing younger ones say, "I can't" or "Do I have to?"

Show you have staying power. A resume with many lateral transfers, or jumps from one company to another without a substantial promotion, indicates people who have trouble committing themselves to the job at hand. Old dinosaurs know this, and they like people who stick with jobs whether they're difficult or easy.

7. *Take care of business—your own.* Be assertive but not pushy. Learn to speak to old dinosaurs from their value systems, not yours. Nobody ever got a raise or promotion because he or she needed it. When you state your case, make sure you make it clear what's in it for the company to promote you or give you more money. They already know what's in it for you.

Know how to ask for a raise. Usually the best time to do it is when you're assigned a new task with more responsibility. Ask whether this carries with it a commensurate increase in pay, or make a deal with the old dinosaurs: "I'll do this for you if you'll raise my pay to this."

This approach can seem mercenary, and if you have any question about how it's done in your company, check it out. Ask what the criterion of success for the new position might be. Once you have clearly met that criterion, then you can ask for more money.

Don't ever ask for a raise by saying, "You gave Joe a raise and he's been here less time than I have." Worse yet is reading the book of job descriptions and "discovering" you were misclassified. (In government positions this is almost the only way to get a raise, but it should be done with the knowledge and approval of your supervisor.)

In general, ask for what you want and, if the answer is no, accept it. You *can* ask what has to change or find out what you have to do to get what you want. Don't gripe because you think you should have something and aren't getting it.

Often it's a good idea to ask for advice about career paths. If you do that, know that you're asking someone to play a mentor role for you and you're pretty well bound to take the advice or risk alienating the person who gave it to you. Remember that this is not a casual question. Many companies have career counselors or employee assistance workers who are outside of the formal power structure and may be the appropriate people for bouncing off ideas about career paths.

8. *Be normal.* Act and dress like the successful people in your company. I don't care what it says in *GQ* or *Cosmopolitan*, wear what the people in your company wear. Having a trademark in clothing or behavior can pay off, but it's a clear boast. A trademark is arrogant behavior, so make sure you can back up the boasting with performance.

Usually it's best to avoid unusual dress or behavior until you've arrived. Worst of all, don't horn in on somebody else's trademark. Don't carry a .357 magnum unless you're Dirty Harry. If the boss wears a bow tie, make sure you wear a nice, conservative four-in-hand.

There are many other aspects of appearing normal, and to do this, you have to know the culture of your company. For example, in many organizations, to get to the top you have to demonstrate that you're a workaholic. The only people who are promoted are those who work Saturdays. If you're in a company like this, it will probably do you no good to point out the injustice of it or argue that people should be rewarded for spending some time with their families or being balanced individuals. If you want the promotion, show up on Saturdays or find another company that has different criteria.

Another important part of being normal is knowing the difference between a business conversation and recreational conversation. Take your cue from the top people. I've known several women who were invited or demanded to go to an Old Boys' Network type of function, a power lunch, golf game or fishing trip, and made themselves outsiders by insisting on talking business.

Above all, don't discuss your personal problems at work. Your boss is not your mother or best friend. You may have a few close friends in your department with whom you can share intimacies, but never make the mistake of seeing your boss as one of those friends. You might need to inform your boss about some problem, a divorce or health trouble, but always let him or her know that you have the situation under control, you're doing something about it, and it won't affect your job for very long. Talking about personal problems with the boss is often seen as making excuses for why you can't do the job or betraying weakness. Old dinosaurs like the strong, silent types.

9. *Take it, but don't dish it out.* Young dinosaurs are rarely allowed to lose their tempers. Keep your cool. It is extremely bad form to get angry at your subordinates or engage in a personality clash with someone you supervise. Teasing and joking from above can be kindly, but never tease someone above you in the hierarchy unless your teasing is clearly flattery, such as "What does an old battle-scarred veteran like you know about the competition?"

A sense of humor can be an important asset, but make sure your joking is not a disguised attack and that the person you're joking about can take it. Humor, like any other art, should be practiced, refined and extremely well done before you think of displaying it outside your home.

10. *Know your place.* Know the structure in your company. Know who's in and who's out. Know who's the power behind the throne. Treat everyone with respect. There is no one whose feelings you can afford to hurt. Know the procedures and rules. If anything is written about your company—a magazine article, policies and procedures manual, court decision or whatever—read it, and know it backward and forward.

Know which group you're a member of and which group you aspire to join. This is especially important for women executives. It's all too easy for women to get into conversations with the secretaries if there are no other women on the management team. This is probably a mistake. To be seen as a manager, you must act like a manager. It's good to help other women in the company develop their careers, but don't take too many lunches with the girls unless you want to be seen as merely one of the girls.

How do you know what the structure and rules are in your company? How do you know who's in and who's out, whom to listen to, and who the up-and-comers are? We're back to the first and most important of these ten commandments: Listen. No matter how difficult it is, listen.

29

Labor and Management

Labor and management are one of those two-category systems that the Dinosaur Brain so delights in perceiving: a system that breaks down into "good" and "evil." Of course, which is good and which is evil depends on which side you're on. When we talk about labor and management we immediately think of organized labor, but we could as easily be talking about hourly and salaried partners and associates, upstairs and downstairs, or any other way of indicating the division between the controllers and the controlled.

Business has dealt with the two sides as if they were adversaries, and the resulting relationship costs billions of dollars a year. There always seems to be a war going on.

In many companies, the assumption seems to be that what's good for labor is bad for management, and vice versa. Each side tends to believe that the other wants to subvert the resources of the company for its own ends.

Management's typical view of labor is that it wants as much money for as little work as possible, and if there's any way to pad the budget, goof off or expect something for nothing, labor will find it.

Labor tends to view management as trying to squeeze out the last little drop of effort for the least amount of pay, so that management can draw huge salaries for sitting around, directing people to do what they don't know how to do themselves.

Each side firmly believes that it's doing all the work. In the companies where I consult, I keep running into the same ideas, stories and beliefs that keep the labor and management conflict going. In each company I'm assured these assumptions reflect reality. Yet they carry the marks of reality distorted to fit the demands of the Dinosaur Brain. What is really true? For my money, it should be what works best.

I am amazed at how often labor and management tend to see the other as incompetent. At whatever level on either side, the pervasive belief seems to be that the real problem is that many of the people on the other side are incompetent and that some of the worst have gravitated to positions of leadership. The two sides reject the basic fact that these people must have been competent at something to have gotten where they are, whether they're union officers or corporate executives.

Each side also tends to assume that the other is evil, that the other would lie, cheat or steal to gain advantage. Neither feels that it's important to understand what the other side does, or what its responsibilities include because, of course, any idiot could do it.

The two groups are typically members of different social classes. They dress differently, act differently, participate in different pastimes, go to different churches and drive different kinds of cars. Everywhere you look, the differences are clearer than the similarities. The Dinosaur Brain always assumes that there is a basic character flaw in people whose values differ from its own.

The Dinosaur Brain defines labor and management as enemies and dictates the strategy in the "war." Each side tends to assume that the only way to deal with these birds is to take a firm stand, because the one group is just waiting to exploit the other.

They both seem to believe that deterrence is the only strategy that makes any agreement possible, that management agrees to terms because it's afraid of a strike and that labor agrees to terms because the members are afraid of losing their jobs. There is a lot of rhetoric on both sides about the terrible things that can happen if you don't deal firmly with the enemy.

Information is "managed." This is a polite way of saying that the two sides tend to lie to each other or conceal important information, feeling that, if the other side had it, it would misuse it. Information is often the main weapon in this war.

Each side tends to talk about the other by using anecdotes that illustrate what "everybody already knows": the atrocities the other side has committed; the managers' monumental salaries; the laborers who spend the whole day drinking and playing poker behind stacks of boxes. Neither side makes much effort to look at a balanced picture.

When labor and management get together, you can be sure it's to thrash out a contract dispute, grievance or similar conflict.

The above assumptions, beliefs and behaviors are pure Dinosaur Brain and are the ways that people who are fighting a war view each other. The mutual antagonism is as old as the dinosaurs.

The Dinosaur Brain says, "Escalate! Drop the big one now! It's time to break the union!" or "It's time to bring management to its knees with that big strike we've been talking about!" The Dinosaur Brain always fights fire with fire, even when water might be more effective.

Perhaps it's time to do something about the lizards around the bargaining table. Many American companies are beginning to see that the war between labor and management is a major factor inhibiting our competitiveness in world markets. Something has to be done. But what?

Some companies are beginning to use their corporate cortex to deal with the problem. They realize that in this struggle, changes in thinking must precede peace talks. Here are some of the changes in attitude and action that can lead to detente:

Develop a "One-Company Mentality." This policy must include a set of overriding rules or ethics that are binding on everyone. If anyone is above the law, there is no law. Seeing management as a service to, rather than a control on, those who are managed will go a long way in this direction. The customer service model that we discussed in Chapter 16 applies here.

Assume That Each Side Has Value and Competence. Make an effort to see things from the other group's point of view. It might be valuable for company executives to learn to operate machinery on the production floor, or answer the PBX or work at some of the other jobs for which they hire union members. Unions should see this as a positive step and try to facilitate it. Union representatives can also be involved in management decision-making and training.

Forgive People for Acting in Their Own Self-Interest. Learn something about the other group's values and make an effort to treat them as legitimate concerns instead of something to be parodied.

Make the Boundaries That Separate the Two Groups More Permeable. Give union members access to training and opportunities that could make them managers. Encourage promotion from within.

Share Information. At its most basic, this means letting other people know what you know. Obviously, when two groups lie to each other, there is no possibility of working together. Involve labor representatives in the planning process and give them a voice in setting corporate goals.

Encourage Labor and Management to Ask Each Other for Mutual Aid and Support. Structure positive communication instead of meeting only to settle disagreements. People who are part of the same herd help each other.

Focus on the Need for Defense from Outsiders, Rather Than from Within. Foster the feeling that the competition is out there, not in here. Emphasize the fact that everyone has something to gain when the company is doing well.

The point at which the labor-management system falls down in most companies is at the level of first-line managers and shop stewards. These tend to be the positions that people would not take by choice; all they can expect is pain and distrust. The shop steward might accept the job out of dedication, a belief in the union's values or a desire to help others, but there is really nothing concrete in it for him or her. The situation is even worse for first-line managers. These people are probably the most disenfranchised, with no one to represent them, little training, least job security and least value within the management structure. Yet they're the ones with the day-to-day contact with the union members and the responsibility for implementing management's philosophy. These are the managers who have the grievances filed against them. Usually a line supervisor is told to see that the job gets done and to make sure that the people above him or her hear as little as possible about what's going on.

It could be beneficial to train shop stewards and first-line supervisors together. These groups, standing on opposite sides of the barricades, have a great deal in common. The more they see about their commonalities, the more smoothly the entire system will operate.

A company at which there are outsiders and insiders isn't functioning as a single herd and will have many difficulties and conflicts, some of which are preventable.

30

The Customer from Outer Space

If you want your clients to keep coming back, make sure they don't feel stupid. Nobody would disagree with this comment, yet more and more clients and customers feel stupid every day. What's going on?

To do business with us, we often require our clients to learn our language, complete with acronyms and abbreviations. The Dinosaur Brain communicates only with insiders. If you're not in the herd, what could you possibly know? If customers don't know our language, they feel ignorant and confused. If you've ever talked to someone who works extensively with computers, you know how it feels to doubt your own intelligence.

If clients are confused, they either must trust us completely or find someone else who communicates better.

Have you ever been lost in a foreign country? I feel that way in an auto parts store. I had to go into one to get one of those little things with a lever and a spring that goes next to the carburetor.

"The what?!" the counterman said when I described it. The look on his face said, "Oh, man. Here's another one of those jerks who works on his own car."

If there was any doubt that he didn't want my business, he made his feelings crystal clear by taking three phone calls while he was supposedly waiting on me. During each conversation, I was left to stare at the little sign on his desk that showed all these guys laughing at me, the customer, because "I Want It When."

My feeling of being lost didn't end there. My next stop was my doctor's office, where he explained some test results. He said:

"The elevation of cholesterol and triglycerides indicates a marginal case of hyperlipidemia. The part I'm most concerned about is the unfavorable ratio of low-density to high-density lipoproteins. This probably indicates a preponderance of saturated fatty acids in the diet, which you'll have to strictly control, because it definitely elevates your risk of coronary heart disease."

I was so frightened that I went out and had an extra-large dish of Häagen-Dazs to soothe my nerves.

After the ice cream, I phoned my broker to find out what percentage of my mutual fund is skimmed off the top by the people who run it. She replied:

"Each portfolio pays the company a supplemental distribution fee equal, on an annual basis, to one percent of the aggregate purchase payment for shares sold since inception, including the purchase price of shares transferred from within and without the fund. This, of course, excludes appreciation, reinvested dividends and capital gain distributions."

My eyes were glazing over by then. It sounded like the IRS was writing her material. I was staring at the wall when the phone rang. It was my attorney, wanting to discuss my publishing contract. He postulated:

"You should never execute a contract without the proviso that you retract copyrights given the conditions subsequent that the publishers fail to comply with their promises both stated and unstated at any future time. But you may not need that language because in most states a contract that did not imply that protection would probably be considered unconscionable anyway."

He was right. I didn't need that language. I didn't even know what that language was.

I was feeling pretty stupid by then. Luckily, I had an appointment with my psychologist. I knew she would straighten me out. She said:

"You may think you feel stupid but you're really angry. Your hostility toward authority figures is threatening to you because of unresolved conflicts with your father. You repress these hostile feelings and attempt to appear overly responsible and productive. This is clearly a reaction formation.

"You may sublimate your hostility by writing self-help books that are, I might add, a device to demonstrate your own adequacy thinly disguised as an attempt to help, but you have not resolved the underlying developmental issues."

It seems to me she said I really don't feel stupid—I am stupid.

By the time I left her office, all I was fit for was reruns of "Three's Company." At least they speak English.

Really, none of these people were trying to make me feel stupid. They were merely talking to me in their own language, assuming I would understand. Their language is clear and precise to them, so they assume it will be to me as well.

I, while being very impressed with their intelligence, will probably have to find some dumber people to work with. I just can't understand the bright ones.

How good is your English? How bright do your customers or clients feel when they do business with you?

Turn yourself into the "customer from outer space" and find out. Get up from your desk, go out the door and come back in as a customer from another solar system and see what it feels like. How much do you have to already know about your business in order to do business with you? Does anyone make an effort to explain things?

Look over your published material with alien eyes. Then your memos. Many people discover that, when they think about their jobs, they don't really think in English as they thought they did.

Want to know how you sound?

Pretend a friend or co-worker is the prospective client from another planet. Your alien customer speaks English but knows nothing of Earth culture or economy. All you have to do is explain what you do and how someone might use your services. You might get into conversations like this:

You: "I'm a stockbroker. I sell shares of stock in public companies to individual and institutional investors."

Alien customer: "What does sell mean? What does a share look like? How do you know what to charge?"

Or

You: "We write liability insurance policies for businesses and professionals."

Alien: "What is liability? What is insurance? And, while you're at it, why are your rates so high?"

Or

You: "I'm an attorney. I . . . oh, never mind."

This little game can provide a quick check on how you sound to the outside world. Consider the advantages of listening carefully to how your client talks about what he or she wants. Language can tell you a lot about what your customer knows. You might even try to get information by asking, "How much do you know about . . . ?" Then try to explain your job or product by using only the words your customer gives you in his or her description.

If you use the client's language, he or she will see you as intelligent, and the customer will feel intelligent too.

The customer from outer space might even be from your own company. I dare you to explain what jobs like marketing and accounting involve without using jargon or acronyms. It's almost as hard as explaining psychology without psychobabble.

Using the client's language is the essence of good customer service, whether your client comes from Manhattan or Altair IV.

31

Gravity

Gravity is an unfair limitation on our freedom. After all, we had no say in the matter at all; we didn't ask to be this heavy.

Gravity isn't just a personal problem; it's an economic problem as well. Just think of all the dollars wasted every year on fighting gravity. In the airline business alone, changes in the law of gravity could save billions a year. Of course, if we eliminated gravity, it would cut way back on our enjoyment of the out-of-doors, but we could do a lot with those dollars.

Stupid? Of course. Gravity is a natural law, and we can't repeal it. Yet in my practice every day, I hear people making themselves miserable with futile struggles against the natural laws of business and human behavior.

When you fight gravity, you're apt to end up with a busted head. (Isaac Newton didn't say that, but he could have. While we're talking about Newton, what would have happened to his career if he'd followed his Dinosaur Brain and gotten angry at the tree, instead of wondering about why apples fall?) Every job has its gravity, its natural laws: divisions of loyalty, compromises, unfairness—the rules that won't be changed, whether you like them or not.

I'm not talking about social injustices, which we must continue to work on as a group over a long period. I'm talking about the rules that determine how people act in business settings. In a way this whole book is about gravity. Dominance, territoriality, aggression, sex and the like will always be with us. We always have a choice about whether to act on them, but we have no choice about whether these urges exist.

Following are a few corporate laws of gravity about which the corporate universe says to you, "You have two choices here: like 'em or lump 'em. That's just the way things are."

1. *There ain't no justice.* Fairness is a human construct; it doesn't apply to the machinations of the gods or the company. A fundamental rule of business is that the bottom line, rather than the moral or aesthetic value of a particular idea, will dictate corporate decisions.

Companies are for profit, and even the not-for-profit companies are more and more required to be efficient.

The first and often last question asked about any new idea or change is, How much will it cost? You need to realize this, have gravity on your side and be ready with an answer. Better yet, have some idea about how your proposed change will make money or save money over a period of time. I'm a firm believer in the long-term view and idea that good ethics make good business. It is still up to me to demonstrate my contentions are correct rather than expecting people to accept my ideas because they are Right.

Opportunities go not to the most qualified but to the people who promote themselves the best and are in the right place at the right time. This may be unfair, but it is definitely not accidental. If you want to get anywhere, you have to learn how to promote yourself and to keep looking for the right place and time.

There will be a lot of people who don't play by the rules, and absolutely nothing happens to them.

Try as you might, you may not be able to motivate anybody to curtail his or her activities or see that anyone gets a well-deserved comeuppance. This presents you with a moral dilemma: Does the fact that somebody else got away with illegal or immoral behavior mean that you have the right to do it too? Does the lack of enforcement make it somehow less immoral? I certainly can't answer that question for you, but I can say that if virtue isn't its own reward, it's probably not rewarded at all.

2. *Nothing ever happens the way it's supposed to*. Count on the fact that your job will change. You will always have to do things that aren't in your job description just to be allowed to do the things that are.

All instructions that you will ever be given will leave out at least one or two crucial items.

Many of the most important questions will never be answered.

3. *People will not do what they should do*. The rules that you follow are not necessarily those that the universe follows.

People will do what they are sufficiently rewarded to do. (This is where virtue being its own reward comes in.) Or they will do what is easiest. A corollary to this is, tasks that are not checked will not be done. Most people will leave most things until the last minute. If there is no time limit, then the task will await judgment day for completion.

4. *People will consider their own feelings and best interests before they consider yours*. This is true even of close friends and family.

Never assume malicious intent when ignorance is sufficient to explain.

People will come to you for favors but will not be as ready to do favors for you when you come to them as you were to do favors for them when they came to you.

People will tell you their problems but will never be available to listen to yours.

If you tell somebody at work something in confidence and it's of any importance, it will get out.

If you are abrasive and aggressive, nobody will ever come and tell you. That's because they're afraid of you.

If you want to form an alliance, make a group cohesive or start a friendship, you will have to do all the work. It will seem that you're the one who always has to do all the phone calling, planning or grunt stuff. If you feel that way, it means you're doing it right.

If you're on a committee, you'll have to do most of the work, but you'll have to divide the credit.

5. *Wherever there are people, there will be politics.* That's really what this book is about. The Dinosaur Brain thinking is the source of politics. You might as well know the rules because you will have to live by them.

6. *There will never be a time of smooth sailing.* As soon as one crisis is over, another will move in to take its place. Nature abhors a vacuum. There will never be a good, quiet time to make a change. If you're waiting for all your work to be done before you take a vacation or do long-term planning, you'll probably wait forever. (This is the problem that workaholics have. It's not, as popularly believed, that they like to work all the time; they're just waiting until the work in front of them is done before they stop.)

7. *The federal government was not created to make your job easier or more efficient.* I think that's enough said about that.

8. *All the information will never be in.* You'll never know in advance whether a decision is right or wrong. Most often you have to choose one of the roads and make it the right choice by your actions after the decision is made.

There are no guarantees. We all have to jump into the darkness. With any luck, Søren Kierkegaard might be there to catch us.

These are some of the natural laws that I've run across. I'm sure there are others. You have no choice on these issues, any more than you do about gravity, but if you want to make yourself miserable by worrying about them, go ahead. You're entitled.

32

Habit and Ritual

The dinosaur brain neither has the capacity for, nor believes in, experimentation. Whatever it does is to be done the same way every time. This conservatism is both an asset and a liability. Both individual habits and institutionalized habits or rituals must be checked from time to time to see if they are working for us or against us.

The Persistence of Habit

Dinosaurs are creatures of habit, and their brains have a way of elevating habits to truths. A lizard will do the same thing in the same way for the same reason, until his habit becomes the only way to do it. If you don't believe me, just think of how you felt, riding in the carpool, when the driver decided to take a slightly different route to work.

When it was your turn to drive again, you probably still took your own route, even if the other way was shorter and had fewer stoplights. Once we have learned habits, we don't question them; we revere them.

Until you really think about it, you don't realize how much time you spend flying on automatic pilot. Once you've learned a complicated sequence, such as riding a bicycle or operating a business machine, you don't keep talking to yourself about what you're doing; you just do it.

Habits are much more efficient than thinking through the same series of actions again and again; you don't have to keep reinventing the wheel. Relying too much on habits, however, can send you into a rut of boredom and inflexibility.

Individuals aren't the only creatures of habit. Groups can get into ruts too. For instance, think about the pattern of your regular departmental meeting. Does it follow the same order each time? Can you predict who's going to sit where and who will say what; which issues will be brought up; who will object to everything and who will agree with everything everybody else says?

Or, consider office procedures. How do you order new equipment? How are people evaluated? How is it decided who gets paid what?

Usually, the first way something is done is the way it always will be done. If you've decided it's time to break an individual or group habit at work, remember that your Dinosaur Brain will assure you that your habit is the one true way. What can your cortex do?

You can use the empirical approach, which involves observing and taking measurements, rather than acting on faith. The empirical approach is the basis of science; the Dinosaur Brain has a strong tendency to act on faith. Faith can be a wonderful thing, but sometimes it's just not efficient.

In the empirical approach, you set goals, test your hypotheses and make plans accordingly. The Dinosaur Brain will urge you to "just do it" because it seems right and fits what you already know. If you follow the Dinosaur Brain, it's not possible to learn anything new from a situation.

Here's how to make an empirical business decision:

   1. *Set a goal.* What do you want to happen?

   2. *Establish criteria.* How will you know if what you wanted to happen has happened?

3. *Think of possibilities and alternative ways of reaching the goal.* When you can see the alternatives, your cortex is working. The Dinosaur Brain never knows from alternatives.

4. *Pick several alternatives and try them.*

5. *Evaluate.* Actually measure results and compare them to your criteria to see which one worked best.

6. *Choose the best solution and use it.*

See what I've done here? I have developed a ritual for cortical thinking, using the Dinosaur Brain tendency to follow step-by-step procedures. Following the steps, however, makes you activate your cortex at each stage. This is the basic pattern of Dinosaur Brains, and it's why I use so many step-by-step approaches. People's Dinosaur Brains want to be told what to do. What I'm really telling you to do is think before you act and you'll be fine, but that doesn't make much of a book.

Now here's one way to make a Dinosaur Brain business decision:

1. *Get an idea from some authority figure,* maybe your boss or some business psychologist, a book or anybody.

2. *Tell everybody that this idea is the basis for all the changes you're going to make.*

3. *Do things the way you've always done them.*

4. *If something good happens, take credit for it.* If something bad happens, point out that it just goes to show that the old ways are best.

The Power of Ritual

Religion has its place in business. I'm not talking about saying your prayers before a merger meeting, but about the power of shared habits or rituals that point to a connection between daily events and something bigger, a connection with other people in the same company doing the same thing for the same reason.

The earliest rituals were ceremonies of transition, habits that symbolized evolutions from one state to another—rites of passage for birth, becoming an adult, joining the tribe, marriage and death. People who participated in the rituals felt a part of something bigger and more powerful than themselves.

Rituals develop at points of change in people's corporate lives—hiring, promotion, transfer and the like. Rituals have power. The way changes are handled communicates strongly about the bond between the person and the company.

Hitler and the Nazi party used ritual better than anyone else in recent years. By their uniforms and ceremonies, their pomp and circumstance, they got an entire country to turn off their cortexes and use their Dinosaur Brains. This surely gives you an idea of the tremendous power of some rituals, for good or evil.

I am not advocating wearing hats or putting on pageants. Just planning. All companies develop rituals, but in most they are understated—such as going to personnel to sign the papers as a rite of passage for promotion. The name of what is happening is seldom spoken, even though what is happening is very important to the person involved. It could be a time for the revealing of new knowledge and fostering a stronger feeling of belonging.

The Dinosaur Brain has a big say in the feeling of being a loyal part of the herd, and it could use some direction. Let's look at a few corporate rituals and see what they communicate and how they might be used.

Joining the Company. When a person joins a company is an excellent time to begin making him or her feel part of the corporate culture. In many companies, the whole hiring experience seems to be designed to conceal what actually goes on from the new person.

It all begins with the job interview. This ritual almost universally involves a mutual sales job. The people in the company tell you how great it is; you tell them how great you are. The underlying rules communicated here are that it's important to withhold certain information because it might create a bad impression and that it's standard procedure to lie for a good cause.

At most companies, new employees have to rely on rumor, gossip and stories to learn how things are actually done, while the formal channels of communications say, "Everyone is equal here; the rules apply to everyone." The grapevine lets you know which people are more equal than others.

The hallmark of dysfunctional corporations is that they don't tell you what the real rules are because the real rules don't sound too good. Instead, people talk about pretend rules and live by the real ones.

Whenever you get a group of people together, you find idiosyncratic and arbitrary rules. That isn't the problem. The problem comes from the pretending that what's going on is not really what's going on. Most of us were inducted into adulthood by families who did the same kind of pretending, so it's easy to understand from the first day on the new job that there are some things one never talks about. Is this the best way to do things?

In your company, isn't it true that certain behaviors are rewarded and certain behaviors definitely are not? Wouldn't it be nice if somebody had told you those things on your first day on the job?

Some companies are experimenting with the Realistic Job Preview technique, in which people are encouraged to tell new or prospective employees what it's really like to work there. This technique can be a powerful means for fostering honesty and building trust. Other companies are experimenting with "boot camp" for new employees, at which an effort is made to induct them into the corporate culture. The emphases are on ceremony and honesty. Old dinosaurs are encouraged to come in and tell stories about how things really are and what to expect.

This kind of ritual can lead to a strong sense of affiliation and the feeling that, from the first, you're enough a part of the herd to be told how things really are.

Needless to say, the Dinosaur Brain would not approve of this boot camp. The Dinosaur Brain believes in hazing, another joining ritual. The idea is that the new members of the herd are so low that they aren't even in the hierarchy yet and they have to be tested to see if they make the grade.

Much of the hazing ritual involves "taking the measure of a person": seeing how far you can push someone to make him angry, where he will draw the line, how good her political instincts are, whether he has a sense of humor or is willing to be deferential. The group can discover all of these things quite quickly by giving the new person a hard time and seeing how he or she handles it. The kind of hard time may differ from the factory floor to the fifty-third floor, but the purpose is the same.

The concept of hazing is universal and could be adapted positively for business. For example, new employees could be expected to do certain tasks and be told at the outset that the purpose is to show their style of working.

This kind of ritual already is in place in academia, where doing a masters thesis or doctoral dissertation is a task that not only shows that you've learned how to do research in a particular area, but also that you've mastered the academic system well enough to be a part of it, that you have the political savvy to actually get the degree.

Status Symbols. No discussion of ritual would be complete without mentioning status symbols. The Dinosaur Brain is always on the lookout for cues about who is on top. The cues are virtually everywhere. What clothes people wear, what they drive, where they eat, what restroom they use, the size and decor of their offices, you name it.

When these cues are displayed, the Dinosaur Brain can be fooled into thinking that one's status is higher than it really is. A great deal of management literature is designed to teach people how to fool the Dinosaur Brain in this way, so much so that large parts of the corporate world wear gray suits, drive gray BMWs and eat lunch at Chez Louis.

The Dinosaur Brain is smarter than that. When everybody has the same, easily visible status symbols, it will pick out more subtle ones that still have meaning. Then there will be more books to read.

Corporate Uniforms. Some companies require corporate uniforms —not the whole outfit, just a jacket, tie, lapel pin or the like. Uniforms are aimed at fostering a sense of esprit de corps, but sometimes they can do just the opposite. If, for example, the CEO doesn't wear the uniform, then wearing it is a mark of being a grunt, and the ritual becomes one of fealty rather than affiliation.

The ritual also goes wrong if wearing the uniform or displaying the object is something you have to do or you get in trouble rather than a choice to show your loyalty or a reward for making the grade. It would be better if the lapel pins could be earned instead of required.

The Change-in-Procedure Ritual. Few companies do this, but the Dinosaur Brain would love a ceremony for burning the old forms, or making the final call on the old phone equipment or turning in the final request on the outdated purchase order. The ritual would reinforce the idea that a new procedure, which will be stressful and difficult at first, has everyone's support and is something the group will take on together.

The Sign-of-Appreciation Ritual. Showing appreciation for significant deeds will become especially important as more companies are legally required to base salaries and promotions on seniority rather than achievement.

Most people will work very hard if they think they have a chance of getting some kind of recognition, such as employee of the month or something similar. It's important, however, for management to be very clear about the requirements for earning the award, because often people aren't clear about the criteria and just assume it's a reward for brownnosing.

Before beginning a mad whirl of staff birthday parties and employee-of-the-month celebrations, however, you need to decide what kinds of behaviors or achievements you're going to reward. They should be the kinds of behaviors you want to see more of: being a team player, showing bravery in the face of adversity, or whatever your company or department holds dear.

A word or two, also, about noncontingent rewards like birthday cakes and Christmas cards from the boss. Once begun, these rituals must be continued or people feel insulted. It's best to keep the ritual manageable from the beginning, a birthday card instead of a cake, for instance, or a sign on the person's office door announcing his or her special day.

Affiliative rewards such as the office party or company picnic can turn into rituals of serfdom if the company doesn't take the time to find out what the rituals mean to the people who have to carry them out. A company picnic, for example, can mean the thing you have to go to and smile during and act like you're having a great time at or else you'll get in trouble with the old man.

The Years-of-Service Ritual. A ritual is only important if it points to something that's really there. If there is no real honor, benefit or gratitude for twenty years of service, then the ritual is hollow and empty. Sometimes a company will try to use a ceremony instead of something real, such as rewarding twenty years of service with more responsibility, more money, a more secure job and more respect within the business community.

Rituals can be an important and positive part of corporate life. To be a positive influence, they must reflect reality, not stand in the place of reality.

33

Management by Mind-Reading: The Case Against Bad Attitude

The supervisor of a large clerical pool once asked me what to do with an employee who had a bad attitude.

"What does she do to give you the idea that she has an attitude problem?" I asked.

"Well," he said, "she's supposed to take typing from three managers. If she feels overloaded, she's supposed to take the typing anyway, then talk to me and I'll negotiate with the people she types for."

"Does she do that?" I asked.

"Well, yes."

"Then what made you think she had a bad attitude?"

The supervisor thought for a minute, then answered. "It's just a feeling you get when you're around her. When she thinks she's overworked, you always know it."

"How do you know it?"

When someone gave the typist what she considered too much work, she would roll her eyes up and expel a large amount of air in an audible sigh. (If you haven't recognized this expression, maybe you could do these two things in front of a mirror and imagine the effect on a supervisor.)

Once we had pinpointed her specific behavior, it was easy to correct this bad attitude. I said to the supervisor, "Tell the typist that the next time someone gives her work to do, she should (1) keep her eyes level, and (2) inhale."

Obviously all attitude problems can't be solved as simply as the typist's, but the story illustrates that an attitude problem is much easier to deal with if you pay more attention to specific behaviors and less to people's attitudes.

Managers can maneuver themselves into having to read their employees' minds when they try to deal with bad attitude. An attitude, by definition, is something inside a person. Unless you're a mind-reader, you have to deduce a person's attitude by something external or objective: what he or she says or does.

Of course, there might be some objective indicators of bad attitude—the typist's rolled eyes and huge sigh, for instance, or a nose in other people's business, horns on the forehead or bared teeth—but for the most part, when a manager believes that an employee doesn't perform well or gets into trouble because of a bad attitude, the manager is relying mostly on guesswork.

When you diagnose someone's attitude, you're really making an inference based on the person's behavior. When you use inferences instead of the behavior itself, you can run into at least three possibilities for error:

   1. You may be incorrect in your inference and misinterpret the meaning of the particular behavior. People can make legitimate mistakes. It's very common for intelligent, talented people to assume that others will be able to do things as well and quickly as they can. When people don't perform as well and quickly, it is often interpreted as if it were purposeful rather than as a real misunderstanding or inability.

To protect against this tendency, it's helpful to have other people walk you through their thought processes so you know just what they understand.

2. You may be correct, but the other person may not be willing to admit that you're right. This can send him or her into Dinosaur Brain thinking and can cause one of the most unproductive kinds of conflict: the "Yes, you are," "No, I'm not" argument.

3. Even if you are correct, and the other person agrees with you, you still haven't given that person any specific behavior or way of thinking to put in place of the bad attitude. You haven't even given the person an opening to talk about the situation without admitting he or she was wrong.

Most jobs are stressful enough that there's no need to provoke unnecessary conflict. When you make inferences about what a person's behavior means, you run the risk of angering him or her. If you can be specific about what you want someone to do, or to stop doing, or, better yet, get him or her to open a dialogue with you, you'll run a far higher chance of getting him or her to comply than if you rely on management by mind-reading.

It's a whole lot easier to say, "Joe, do something about that little attitude problem" than to say, "Joe, since I started supervising your shift, your sick days have tripled. You tap your fingers on the desk when I talk with you. When I comment about your work you usually answer, 'If you say so.' When you do those things, I feel criticized, like you're saying I don't know what I'm talking about. Is that what you intend me to feel?"

In the latter wording, you offer openings to get at the feelings underlying the attitude, to discuss Joe's discontent or to suggest specific changes in his behavior. The basic form for this kind of approach is:

"When you said/did . . ." (be as specific about behavior as possible), "I felt. . . ." (People can't argue that you didn't feel something the way they can if you imply you know what they felt.) "Is that what you intended?" (This gives them an out, a way of changing without losing face.) "I'd like it if you would. . . ." (Be specific about what behavior you want.)

This interchange takes a bit longer than one minute if it's done correctly, but it can save you a lot of difficulty later on.

34

How to Make Your Colleagues Mad at You

Bright-eyed and scaly-tailed, Donald Dinosaur arrived for work, eager to start his busy day. There was much to be done and no time to waste. He checked his appointment book and noted with rage that his secretary had forgotten to list his lunch meeting with the big brontosaurus himself, the CEO.

A livid Donald rushed to the outer office, brandishing the telltale calendar above his secretary's head and yelling, "If you can't even remember to write down my appointments, what am I paying you for? What kind of a moron are you, anyway?" The rest of the staff looked on in sympathy while Donald heaped more abuse on his assistant's bowed head.

Our hero's next stop was the office of the company's chief accountant. Thwack went a pile of papers onto the man's desk. Thump went Donald's fist on top of the pile, to punctuate his greeting. "Gimme these cost analyses, itemized by departments, by 11:30 sharp this morning. No excuses, buddy. On my desk by 11:30. I got a meeting with the big boss at noon and he'll be asking for 'em. Get my drift?" Donald didn't notice the accountant's hostile stare as he slammed the door.

Then Donald marched back to his own cave, humming a merry tune. Heads were rolling, yes sir, and there would be more to come. He had a plan that could put this company on the map, and he'd have the Big

Guy's ear at lunch to get it okayed. No use even bothering to run it by Donald's own supervisor. That wimp wouldn't even give him the time of day. Nope, Donald would go right to the top with this brainstorm.

Before coffee break, Donald had already managed to make half the staff mad at him. By early afternoon, when news of his brainstorm leaked back to his supervisor, Donald would also be in hot water with his boss.

We all know people like Donald. Often we refer to them by using the colloquial name of a bodily orifice and think that the name explains their behavior. We know they can make us angry, but we seldom stop and consider how they do it. The self-help books have been silent. Until now.

Donald acts like a dominant dinosaur by publicly showing aggression against the people in his office. His aggressive behavior tells them he thinks he is so far above them that he can't be challenged. He dares other people's Dinosaur Brains to wage war against him. Most people won't, either because they are a bit lower in the hierarchy or because they have had rudimentary training in manners.

If we don't retaliate against Donald, our Dinosaur Brains say we are admitting that he is correct in his judgment of our status. If we do retaliate, our cortex tells us we face punishment from our peers or from ourselves. It is the internal conflict from this bind that makes us so angry.

Donald's demand implied that he was dominant over the chief accountant. It also said that mere asking would not have been enough to get him to do his job correctly or in a timely way. If Donald had watched the reaction, he would have seen the accountant's outraged glare, which said, "Red alert! Prepare for attack! Fight back!"

The accountant likely would have reacted to Donald's peremptory manner with passive aggression, by burying the asked-for cost analyses under his desk blotter. Donald could be lucky to get the figures by Christmas. (Of course, there is no aggression without retaliation, but why spoil the chief accountant's fun by telling him that?)

Not everybody can be as actively abrasive as Donald. If you're the retiring type, you can still make people just as angry by using any one of these tried and true approaches. If you follow the advice in this chapter, people will refer to you as the same part of the anatomy as Donald. I promise. If people don't get mad at you, let me know and I'll print a retraction.

How to Make Your Co-Workers Angry at You

Talk Behind the Back. You can say the same things Donald does. Just say them to someone else. In an organization, you can be sure that if you say something behind someone's back, he or she will eventually hear about it and find out that you said it. The person will be twice as angry if he or she hears it from someone other than you. You can make him or her three times as angry by denying you said it.

"People are Saying. . . ." A variation on talking behind the back is the old "People are saying" technique. You say to a colleague, "People are saying that you're an idiot." Both of you know who really thinks he or she is an idiot. Your colleague will definitely not appreciate this helpful information and will treat you as if you had started the rumor, whether you did or not. Remember that the Greeks used to kill the bearers of bad news.

The "You Are/You Did" Comment. When people do things that you don't like, there are lots of ways to get them to do things differently. The most effectively enraging is by saying, "You are incompetent, stupid, not management material. . . ." Take your pick. Or point out exactly what they did wrong.

The most blatant form of this technique is name-calling, but that should be reserved only for special occasions. Typically a subtle suggestion that the person is to blame for whatever bad thing has happened is all that's needed. You can be as direct or indirect as you want. Try one of these to get you started:

"Somebody did [name offense the jerk committed] wrong."

"Your department seems to be the bottleneck."

"You've really got an attitude problem."

"You never listen." (Using "you always" and "you never" in front of a comment is a great device for obscuring the specific issue and attacking the person.)

Any sentence that begins with "you are" and does not end with "wonderful" will be experienced as name-calling.

If you ever want action without angering people, it's better to talk more about what you want than what they did or are. It's much more effective to tell people what you want:

"I'd like you to do it this way." (You'd be surprised how few times you actually have to point out a mistake to get people to change their actions. If you do have to point out an error and, for some reason you don't want people to get mad, you can say *you* make the same mistake.)

"Can I have the report by Tuesday?"

"I'd like you to be here by 8:30 every day."

"Let's schedule a few uninterrupted minutes to talk about this. Let's meet again in two weeks to see how far we've gotten with this issue." (Set the stage for listening.)

Public Humiliation. Any of the techniques described here work best in front of a group. A couple of people is best because if the group is too large they can sympathize with the underdog and turn on you. Louis XVI found this out the hard way.

Many things that could be ignored in private become much more insulting when done in public. Interrupting, correcting facts and even strategically omitting someone's accomplishments can effectively push people's buttons when you do them in front of a group.

Call Somebody into Your Office. Do this when everybody knows the only reason you call people in is to chew them out.

How to Make Your Supervisor Angry at You

The Exploitation Play. You can use a demand to suggest that your supervisor is exploiting you or depriving you of something that is yours by right, such as fair wages.

Try this: Get hold of the book of job descriptions and find your supervisor's job. Now go to your supervisor and tell him or her that the job description in the book is really a description of *your* job and that you should be making more money. It doesn't necessarily have to be your supervisor's job. Any one that pays more will do and they all sound the same. I'm not sure whether this technique will get you a raise, but I guarantee it will get you animosity.

Demanding all your rights by the letter of the law and mumbling about stress-claims or discrimination suits also work well in many situations.

The End Run. Donald's lunch meeting with the CEO is a great example of the end run. By deciding to go over his own supervisor's head, Donald made sure that his boss would find out about his grand scheme through the office grapevine, or from the Big Enchilada himself. In either case, Donald's boss loses face.

The end-run strategy is, if your boss won't do something for you, go to your boss's boss and ask him or her to do it. If this nets you what you want, it will mean that the higher boss has moved into the organizational spot occupied by your own supervisor, as if your boss were not there at all. There is no animal in the corporate jungle more dangerous than the bypassed supervisor. You've managed to get him publicly treated as if he didn't exist.

The Refusal. If you want to make any supervisor so angry that he or she can't see straight, all you have to do when you're asked to do something is to answer, "That's not in my job description."

Instant Deafness. One of the best ways to enrage the old slave-driver is just by pretending you didn't hear it when he told you to do something. It's easy and it always works.

How to Make the People You Supervise Angry at You

Pull Rank. Nobody likes direct orders. They point out clearly who is top dinosaur. The more you give, the angrier people will get. A particularly provocative technique is posting a whole new set of procedures in response to someone's mistake. Donald probably will have a memo on the department bulletin board by 11 A.M.: "NOTICE: Any secretary who forgets to list her boss's appointments on his calendar will have to run 17 laps around the parking lot and will lose all accrued sick leave for the year." Why get just one person angry when you can irritate your whole department?

Minimize Experience. The people you supervise have probably been doing their jobs for a number of years. If you imply, by your words or actions, that you know more about doing their jobs than they do, it will be sure to infuriate them. Helpful suggestions, unless phrased very carefully, are seldom helpful. Improvements or changes in procedure initiated from the top without input will always be heard as criticism. The implication is that your subordinates are too dumb to know how to do their jobs.

Imply Moral Turpitude or Dishonesty. Most of the people who work for you are honest and industrious. If you set policies to control the worst of your employees, you will definitely anger your best. Drug testing is one of the best examples of policy that creates far more problems than it solves. In law there is a notion of probable cause. It is important to have some demonstrable reason for believing that particular employees are messing up before you use invasive techniques to check up. If not, the message of distrust will be heard loud and clear, especially by the people who are most trustworthy.

Forget. The simplest techniques are always the best. Forgetting anything will let people assume that you don't think it's important enough to remember, especially if you forget all the time.

The Dinosaur Brain is very sensitive to aggression, particularly to the kind that implies that you're the low dinosaur or aren't even worthy of notice. These techniques really work, and the variations are endless. You too can be thought of as a bodily orifice! So what if these strategies always elicit retaliation? You're no wimp. You can take it, can't you?

Afterword

The great beast leans back in repose as he takes a few moments to digest the material from this book. His reverie is disturbed by a colleague.

"Whatcha eating?"

"Oh, nothing," he says. "Just a book about Joe down the hall."

The Dinosaur Brain is not very good at handling new information. It thinks it already knows the important stuff, and it does. The stuff that's important for surviving in the jungle.

The Dinosaur Brain is very powerful, but without the cortex, it can be extremely dumb. This book has attempted to demonstrate that there is another layer of thinking and experience below the obvious. These patterns of thought and action can take over and run things if you don't pay attention.

Business is too important to run on automatic pilot. Dinosaur Brain patterns, untempered by cortical reasoning, lead to inefficiency, waste and, most of all, stress. Your job is undoubtedly stressful enough that you don't need to manufacture any more tension for yourself.

In this book we have offered a number of different views of conscious and unconscious thinking and countless lists of things to do in different situations. We have now reached the end, and it seems appropriate to try to sum up the whole message.

When you're motivated, excited and enthusiastic, you can be sure that your Dinosaur Brain is working. You may want to just go with these feelings and not spoil them by analyzing them too much, or you may decide to use your cortex to find out what leads to your motivation and enthusiasm so that you can return to these states of mind at will.

When you're irritated, frustrated and stressed out, you can also be sure that your Dinosaur Brain is operating. Whatever the emotions, you know there's Lizard Logic involved.

What do you do? First, stop. Get the big picture. The Dinosaur Brain has no perspective at all. Shift to your cortex. Ask yourself, "What do I want to happen?" Choose your actions according to your goal. Think about how you are going to make it happen. As you are acting, ask yourself, "Am I getting closer or farther away from the goal?"

All you have to do is stop and think. If you do that, then you can be in control of an enormous primeval force within you, rather than having that force control you.

Keep your cortex working when you go back to the jungle. Even if you aren't the biggest, meanest and most powerful dinosaur, you can easily be the smartest. In the end, the smartest wins.

Suggested Readings

Ardrey, R. *The Social Contract: A Personal Inquiry into the Evolutionary Sources of Order and Disorder*. New York: Atheneum, 1970. More thoughts on man's (and woman's) instinctive underpinnings.

Ardrey, R. *The Territorial Imperative*. New York: Atheneum, 1966. Widely known and respected work on the genetic instinctive bases of aggression.

Buber, M. *Good and Evil*. New York: Scribners, 1952. Classic philosophical work on the religious views of right and wrong, good and evil.

Elgin, S. H. *The Gentle Art of Verbal Self-Defense*. New York: Prentice-Hall, 1980. A book on the intricacies of verbal combat. Points out clearly that what you say and how you say it are very important.

Freudenberger, H. J., and Richelson, G. *Burnout*. New York: Doubleday, 1980. One of the best books written on job stress. Explains why some of the stress you feel in your job really comes from your experience with your family and your past.

Gendlin, E. T. *Focusing*. New York: Bantam, 1978. A gentle and poetic self-help book that describes a powerful technique for getting people in touch with their own feelings. A must-read if you're going to deal effectively with your Dinosaur Brain.

Halberstam, D. *The Reckoning*. New York: William Morrow and Co., 1986. Absorbing history of the American and Japanese auto industries. Some fascinating examples of the destructive potential of Dinosaur Brain management.

Kets deVries, M.F.R., ed. *The Irrational Executive: Psychoanalytic Studies in Management.* New York: International Universities Press, 1984. A series of articles, mostly highly technical, that detail the roles of unconscious forces in everyday management. Hard reading, but worth it.

Kuhn, T. *The Structure of Scientific Revolutions.* Chicago: The University of Chicago Press, 1962. One of the three most significant books I have ever read. Shows that the progress of knowledge, like everything else, is political.

McCormack, M. H. *What They Don't Teach You in Harvard Business School: Notes from a Street-Smart Executive.* New York: Bantam, 1984. A manual of ideas and strategy that shows a good understanding of the notion of the cortex and Dinosaur Brain, although they are not discussed as such. An excellent companion piece to Musashi.

Morris, D. *The Naked Ape.* New York: McGraw-Hill, 1967. Classic popular ethology work. A must for Dinosaur Brain aficionados. Speculation as to the instinctive basis of many common behaviors.

Musashi, M. *A Book of Five Rings: The Classic Guide to Strategy.* Woodstock, N. Y.: The Overlook Press, 1982. If you ever want to engage in conflict, this is how to do it. Written by the fastest sword in seventeenth century Japan.

Sagan, C. *The Dragons of Eden: Speculations on the Evolution of Human Intelligence.* New York: Random House, 1977. Popular statement of the triune brain theory, as well as billions of other interesting ideas.

Scheele, A. *Skills for Success.* New York: William Morrow and Co., 1979. Interesting and balanced ideas about how to succeed in the world of business. Realpolitik.

Sloma, R. S. *No Nonsense Management.* New York: Macmillan, 1977. Well stated and clear, this could be the Dinosaur Brain's book of policies and procedures. As written, it is direct, reasonable and rational, but the words could be used to justify considerable excess.

Tavris, C. *Anger, The Misunderstood Emotion.* New York: Simon and Schuster, 1982. The best book on the subject. Required reading.

Watzlawick, P. *Ultra-Solutions: How to Fail Most Successfully.* New York: W.W. Norton and Company, 1988. Beautifully written, clearly demonstrates how we strive to be miserable even when we could be happy.

Index

Abrasiveness:
  angering colleagues by, 241–242
  in Triple F response, 31
Absentee policy, 202
Acronyms, 224
Adolescents, corporate, 197–205
Advice:
  from mentor, 176–177, 212
  from old dinosaur, 207–208
Affairs, 7, 57–58
  and loneliness, 167
  and mentor relationships, 175–177
  reasons for, 181–186
  stages of, 58–65
  termination of, 65–66
Agenda, hidden, 116–117
Aggressiveness:
  angering colleagues by, 241–242
  and dominance, 38
  and Triple F Response, 31, 32
Alcohol abuse:
  and loneliness, 167
  and office romance, 186
All-American, situation-comedy parent,
    190–191
Ambition, 38
Anecdotes:
  in labor vs. management, 217
  reuse of old, 148
  in self-promotion, 162
Anger:
  in clients, 125–130
  in colleagues, 241–246

in employees, 245–246
positive uses of, 119–124
in supervisor, 244–245
in young dinosaurs, 213
Appreciation ritual, 235–236
Arousal:
  avoidance of, 90
  measurement of, 141–142
  in Triple F Response, 27–35
Attention span, 149
Attitude:
  bad, 237–239
  positive, 143–144
Authority:
  delegation of, 172
  and motivation, 139
  territoriality and, 48
Avoidance, 5, 27–28, 32–34

Bad attitude, 237–239
Bad moods, 95–97
Banter, 59
Behavior, inferences about, 238–239
Benign neglect, 52
Birthday parties, 235–236
Blaming, 7–8, 67–68
  corporate-level, 68–69
  personalized, 69–72
  what to do about, 73–75
  with "you are/you did" comment, 243
Blind-side attack, 115–118
Blood pressure, 142
Boot camp, 233

Boredom:
  and impulsiveness, 19–20, 24
  and loneliness, 166–167
  with out-of-shape mind, 148
Boss, angering of, 244–245
Brushfire management:
  and impulsiveness, 4, 17, 19–20
  vs. long-term planning, 151, 155
Bugs Bunny strategy, 193
Burnout syndrome, 83–84
  in corporate juvenile delinquents, 201
  and office romance, 185

Captain Kirk management style, 48,
    171–172
Career, job vs., 198–200
Career paths, 212
Challenge, and stress, 142–143, 144
Changes in routine:
  irritation at, 147–148, 149
  ritual for, 235
Children, corporate, 188, 191
Christmas cards, 235–236
Citizen, good, 209
Clarity, 18–19
Classification systems, 8, 77–79
  and burnout syndrome, 83–84
  of labor vs. management, 215–217
  with out-of-shape mind, 148–149
  in personality clash, 79–80
  with workaholic ethic, 80–83
  and wrong job, 84–86
Clients:
  angry, 125–130
  from outer space, 221–224
Closure, 29–30
Clothing, 212, 234–235
Cognitive set, 10
Commands, 136, 245–246
Commitment:
  in dealing with old dinosaurs, 211
  and employee motivation, 139
  and stress, 142, 144
  to wrong job, 85–86
Communication:
  with client, 221–224
  opening of closed, 121
Compassion, 117
Competence, 216, 218
Competitiveness:
  blaming and, 69
  and dominance, 38, 42–44
  in junior shark tanks, 203–204
  in labor vs. management, 217, 218
  in long-term planning, 155–156
Complaining, 7, 67, 72–73
  to old dinosaurs, 209
  what to do about, 73–75
Compliments, 193
Concentration, 149
Confiding, 60
Consistency, 137

Content, 114
Control:
  and blaming, 71
  and stress, 142, 143–144
  over thoughts, 95–97
Conversation, business vs. recreational, 213
Coping techniques, 143–146
Corporate mother, 191–192
Corporate style, 41
Cortex, 3, 4
  vs. dinosaur brain, 9–14
Courtship, 7, 57–58
  and loneliness, 167
  and mentor relationships, 175–177
  reasons for, 181–186
  stages of, 58–65
  termination of, 65–66
Crabbiness, 99–105
  at changes in routine, 147–148
Creative ignoring, 74
Crises, 228
Crisis management:
  and impulsiveness, 4, 17, 19–20
  vs. long-term planning, 151, 155
Criticism:
  and impulsiveness, 24
  and manipulation, 108
Crying, 109–111
Customer:
  angry, 125–130
  from outer space, 221–224
Customer service model, 55, 131–134

Dad, corporate, 187, 188–190, 191–192
Dark mother, 192–193
Deafness, instant, 245
Debt, implied, 114–115
Decisions:
  corporate-level blame for, 68–69
  information for, 228
  and motivation, 139
Defense of territory, 6, 45–55
Defensive patterns, 5, 27–35
Delay, 30–31
Delegating:
  vs. Captain Kirk management style, 172
  and motivation, 139
  territoriality and, 48
Department size, 54
Depression, 185
Descriptions, in self-promotion, 161
Dinosaur Brain:
  vs. cortex, 9–14
  defined, 3–4
Directness, 18–19
Dishonesty, implication of, 246
Display, 59
Distress call, 114–115
Divorce, 185
Dominance, 5–6, 37–38
  and corporate style, 41
  of mentors, 174, 178

playing to win, 42–44
status vs. leadership, 38–40
territory and, 46–48
Drug abuse:
  and irritability, 105
  and office romance, 186
  and stress, 21
Drug testing, 246
Dynamite, anger as, 121–122

Eccentric uncles, 194
Emotions:
  "excess gas" theory of, 100
  flat, 148
  instincts and, 13
  in manipulation, 109–111
  in office romance, 62
Emphasis, anger for, 120
Empire-building, 6, 45–55
Empirical approach, 230–231
Employees:
  angering of, 245–246
  listening to, 110, 136–137
  motivation of, 135–140
End run, 109, 245
Error, admission of, 130
Ethics, 21–22
Exercise, 150
  mental, 149–150
Experience, minimization of, 246
Expertise, 210
Explanations, 91–92
  to angry clients, 127–128
Exploitation play, 244–245
Expression, personal, 119–120
Eye contact, 210

Fairness, 139, 226–227
Familiarity, in office romances, 182–183
Families, corporate, 187–195
Fantasy:
  in office romance, 60
  in Triple F Response, 29–30
Father, corporate, 187, 188–190, 191–192
Favorite sons, 194
Fight response, 5, 27–28, 30–32
Fighting back, 91
  with angry client, 126–127
First-line managers, 218–219
Flat emotions, 148
Flattery, 193
Flight response, 5, 27–28, 32–34
Follow-through:
  vs. impulsiveness, 18
  in motivation, 137–138
Forgetting:
  angering employees by, 246
  as flight response, 32
Forgiveness, 74
Friendliness, 208–209
Friends, 165–170
Fright response, 5, 27–28, 34–35

Frustration, 30–31
Futurist book, 155

Gift giving:
  in manipulation, 114–115
  in office romance, 61
Giving and taking:
  in burnout syndrome, 83–84
  in manipulation, 114–115
Goals:
  and impulsiveness, 24
  in long-term planning, 152, 154
  mixed, 128
  and motivation, 137
Godzilla meets Rodan effect, 14
Going over someone's head, 109, 245
Good citizen, 209
Good vs. bad classification, 8, 77–79
  and burnout syndrome, 83–84
  of labor vs. management, 215–217
  with out-of-shape mind, 148–149
  in personality clash, 79–80
  with workaholic ethic, 80–83
  and wrong job, 84–86
Gossip, 72
  angering colleagues by, 243
  in manipulation, 116–117

Habit, persistence of, 229–231
Hazing, 233–234
Heart attacks, 20, 80–81
Heart rate:
  and impulsiveness, 23
  monitoring of, 90, 142
Hidden agenda, 116–117
Hierarchies, 5–6, 37–44
High blood pressure, 142
Hiring process, 232–234
Hiss response, 7–8, 67–75
History, of company, 152–153, 204–205
Hostility:
  angering colleagues by, 241–242
  and dominance, 38
  and Triple F Response, 31, 32
Humiliation, public, 138–139, 244
Humor:
  in dealing with old dinosaurs, 213
  and stress, 144
Hunger, 104
Hypnosis, 144–146

Ignoring, creative, 74
Illness:
  in corporate juvenile delinquent, 201–202
  as Triple F Response, 32
Image assessment, after office romance, 65–66
Imagery, 144–146
Impatience, 19–20, 21
Implied debt, 114–115
Impulsiveness, 4, 17–25
Incentives, 140

Incompetence, 216, 218
Indispensability, 210
Inferences, about behavior, 238–239
Information:
　for decisions, 228
　between labor and management, 217, 218
Instant deafness, 245
Instincts, 13
Interest, limited areas of, 148
Internal television, 95–97
Interview, job, 232
Intimidation, 107–109
Irritability, 99–105
　at changes in routine, 147–148

Jargon, 224
Job:
　vs. career, 198–200
　wrong, 84–86
Job descriptions:
　angering supervisor with, 244–245
　changes in, 227
Job interview, 232
Job openings, 162
Job title, 46
Job training, 139, 140
Junior shark tank, 203–204
Justice, 139, 226–227
Juvenile delinquents, corporate, 197–205

Knowing your place, 213–214

Labor, vs. management, 139, 215–219
Language, of client, 221–224
Laws of business, 225–228
Leadership, 38–40, 42–43
Listening:
　to angry client, 128–129
　to employees, 110, 136–137
　and mental sluggishness, 149–150
　to old dinosaurs, 207–208
Lizard Logic, 4–8
Loneliness, 165–170
Long-term planning, 151–156
Losing your cool, 111–114

Making waves, 157–163, 226
Making you look bad, 111–114
Management:
　vs. labor, 139, 215–219
　by mind-reading, 237–239
　of self, 151–153
Manipulation strategies, 107
　attack from the blind side, 115–118
　implied debt, 114–115
　intimidation and the emotional scene,
　　107–111
　trying to make you look bad, 111–114
Married lovers, 64–65, 184
M*A*S*H units, 202–203
Meetings:
　midnight, 19, 155
　in office romance, 60

Mental aerobics, 149–150
Mental sluggishness, 147–150
Mentor relationship, 173–179, 212
Midnight meetings:
　and impulsiveness, 19
　in long-term planning, 155
Military model, 136
Mind, out-of-shape, 147–150
Mind-reading, management by, 237–239
Mistake, admission of, 130
Monitoring system, 138
Moods, bad, 95–97
Moralistic patriarch, 188–190
Moral judgments, 8, 77–79
　and burnout syndrome, 83–84
　of labor vs. management, 215–217
　with out-of-shape mind, 148–149
　in personality clash, 79–80
　with workaholic ethic, 80–83
　and wrong job, 84–86
Moral turpitude, implication of, 246
Mother:
　corporate, 191–192
　dark, 192–193
Motivation:
　anger for, 120–121
　of employees, 135–140
　unconscious, 10–12
Muscle tension, 142

Name association, 161
Name-calling, 243, 244
Natural laws, 225–228
Negative thoughts, 95–97
Neglect, benign, 52
Negotiation, 93
New ideas, irritation at, 147–148
New-ideas department, 203
Normal behavior, 212–213
Noticing stage, of office romance, 58–59

Obnoxiousness, 107
Office party, 236
Office politics, 228
Office romances, 7, 57–58
　and loneliness, 167
　and mentor relationships, 175–177
　reasons for, 181–186
　stages of, 58–65
　termination of, 65–66
Old Boy network:
　conversation in, 213
　and job vs. career, 199
　and loneliness, 165, 166
Old dinosaurs, dealing with, 207–214
On-again, off-again stage, of office
　romance, 63–64
One big happy family, 187–195
One-company mentality, 217–218
Orders, 136, 245–246
Outer space, customer from, 221–224
Outings, 236

Out-of-shape mind, 147–150
Overload, 23

Paranoia, 69
    reverse, 32
Paraphrasing, 129
Parents, corporate, 187–195
Parties, 236
Patriarch, moralistic, 188–190
"People are saying" technique, 243
Perfectionism, 81
Personal expression, anger for, 119–120
Personality clash, 79–80
Personal problems, 213
Personal space, 46–48
Petitions, 109
Picnics, 236
Planning, long-term, 151–156
Playing by the rules, 226–227
Politics, 228
Positive attitude, 143–144
Possessiveness, 61–62
Power, in empire-building, 50–51
Power struggles, 5–6, 37–44
Praise, 140
Premenstrual tension, 100, 103–105
Presentations, in self-promotion, 162
Priorities:
    in long-term planning, 151–152
    and Triple F Response, 33–34
    and workaholic ethic, 83
Private practice, self-promotion in, 158
Procedural changes:
    irritation at, 147–148, 149
    rituals for, 235
Process, 114
Procrastination, 32
Professionals, self-promotion by, 158
Profitability, 226
Promotion:
    and motivation, 139
    and self-promotion, 159–163, 226
Public humiliation, 138–139, 244
Public speaking, 35
Pulling rank, 245–246
Pulse rate:
    and impulsiveness, 23
    monitoring of, 90, 142
Putting out fires:
    and impulsiveness, 4, 17, 19–20
    vs. long-term planning, 151, 155

Questions:
    in manipulation, 113–114, 117, 118
    to old dinosaurs, 209–210

Raise, asking for, 211–212
Realistic Job Preview technique, 233
Reality:
    and personalized blame, 69–70
    in Triple F Response, 29–30
Real Thing, vs. office romance, 183–186

Rebel without a cause, 200–201
Recognition ritual, 235–236
Refusal, 245
Relaxation techniques, 24, 144–146
Releasers, 13
Reptile Response, 11
    avoidance of, 89–94
Research department, 203
Respect:
    anger as, 121
    and motivation, 139
Restating, 92
    with angry clients, 129
Retreats, 152, 154
Reverence, 209
Reverse paranoia, 32
Rewards:
    and motivation, 140
    sign-of-appreciation ritual, 235–236
Ridicule:
    and manipulation, 108–109
    and motivation, 138–139
Right job, 84–86
Right vs. wrong classification, 8, 77–79
    and burnout syndrome, 83–84
    of labor vs. management, 215–217
    with out-of-shape mind, 148–149
    in personality clash, 79–80
    with workaholic ethic, 80–83
    and wrong job, 84–86
Risk taking:
    and blame, 69
    in junior shark tank, 203–204
Rituals, 231–236
Romance, 7, 57–58
    and loneliness, 167
    and mentor relationships, 175–177
    reasons for, 181–186
    stages of, 58–65
    termination of, 65–66
Routine, changes in, 147–148, 149, 235
Rules of business, 225–228
Running away:
    from angry client, 127
    by explaining, 91
    in Triple F Response, 5, 27–28, 32–34

Safety, of office romance, 183
Saving face, 130
Scenes, emotional, 109–111
Scheduling:
    in long-term planning, 151–152
    and Triple F Response, 33–34
    and workaholic ethic, 83
Self-descriptions, 161
Self-hypnosis, 144–146
Self-management, 151–153
Self-promotion, 157–163, 226
Sell, don't tell, 136
Selling oneself, 157–163, 226
Separation, marital, 185
Sexual harassment, 183

Sexual relationship, 7, 57–58
   and loneliness, 167
   and mentor relationships, 175–177
   reasons for, 181–186
   stages of, 58–65
   termination of, 65–66
Shark tank, 203–204
Shop stewards, 218–219
Shyness, 209
Sickness:
   in corporate juvenile delinquents,
      201–202
   as Triple F Response, 32
Sign-of-appreciation ritual, 235–236
Situation-comedy parent, 190–191
Smiling, 208
Socializing:
   and loneliness, 165–170
   and motivation, 139–140
Sons, favorite, 194
Space, personal, 46–48
Speaking, public, 35
Specialty area, 210
Stage fright, 5, 27–28, 34–35
Status:
   vs. leadership, 38–40
   in office romances, 183
Status symbols, 234
Stories:
   in labor vs. management, 217
   reuse of old, 148
   in self-promotion, 162
Straight arrow, 66
Stress, 141–142
   coping with, 143–146
   in corporate juvenile delinquents, 201
   problems related to, 20–21
   in stress-hardy individuals, 142–143
Stupidity, of customers, 221–224
Style, corporate, 41
Subordinates:
   angering of, 245–246
   listening to, 110, 136–137
   motivation of, 135–140
Supervisor, angering of, 244–245
Sympathetic response, 27–28

Teaching, 150
Team players:
   vs. blaming, 69
   vs. competitiveness, 38, 40, 204
   and old dinosaurs, 209
Teasing, 213

Teenagers, corporate, 197–205
Telephone calls, in office romance, 60–61
Television, internal, 95–97
Territoriality, 6, 45–55
Territorial markers, 45, 46
Territory:
   with office romance, 63
   and personal space, 46–48
Thinking:
   control over, 95–97
   out-of-shape, 147–150
Threat, 5, 27–35
Time management:
   in long-term planning, 151–152
   and Triple F Response, 33–34
   and workaholic ethic, 83
Time pressure, 30–31
Title, job, 46
Touching, 61
Trademark, 212
Training, 139, 140
Triple F Response, 5, 27–35
Turf struggles, 6, 45–55
Type A personality:
   and stress, 20
   and Triple F Response, 31

"Uh huh" rule, 91
Uncles, eccentric, 194
Unconscious motivation, 10–12
Unfinished business, 29–30
Uniforms, 234–235
Union, 139, 215–219

Vulnerability, 115–118

Winning:
   and dominance, 42–44
   and Triple F Response, 30, 31, 32
Women:
   irritability in, 99–100, 103–105
   know your place for, 214
   loneliness in, 166
   management style of, 140
Workaholic ethic, 80–83
Wrong job, 84–86

Years-of-service ritual, 236
Yelling, 90–91
   in manipulation, 109–111
"You are/you did" comment, 243–244

Zero-sum fallacy, 38